Fly me to t

By Melanie Arlene Hume

Title ID: 6532568
ISBN 13-978-1537345680
ISBN-10:
1537345680

Author Melanie Arlene Hume
Text copyright Melanie Arlene Hume
Published by CreateSpace.com 2016
All rights reserved.

No part of this publication may be stored in a retrieval system, reproduced or transmitted, in any form or by any means, mechanical, electronic, recording or otherwise, except brief extracts for the purpose of review, with the prior permission in writing from the copyright owner.

I would like to thank the real-life members of those portrayed in this book for being part of my story.
All written content is purely from memory and certain identities are disguised as per legal requirement.
Events detailed in this autobiography are my recollection only and all rights are reserved and copyrighted.

CHAPTER

SYNOPSIS

Chapter 1	Submerged
Chapter 2	The early years
Chapter 3	Low school
Chapter 4	The emancipation of sanity
Chapter 5	Talk the talk
Chapter 6	Freud and fat fashion
Chapter 7	The art of rejection
Chapter 8	Social vortex
Chapter 9	Friars funhouse
Chapter 10	An emotional shift
Chapter 11	Finding motherland
Chapter 12	What is the story mother glory?
Chapter 13	Chapter change
Chapter 14	Start spreading the news
Chapter 15	The Final Chapter: What is the script?

DEDICATION

The journey you are about to indulge in is my life so far. Other writers, my friends and family inspire it.
I dedicate it to a wonderful human, Iain Hume.

Dad, for the struggles you faced, for the strength you embraced and for the person you are, I am blessed to call you my father. This story in all its wonder is inspired by you, is dedicated to you, and you alone.

Thank you

I love you.

1

Submerged

Writing, an extremely challenging yet surprisingly inspiring past time. Writing your autobiography can go one of two ways; you are deemed a narcissistic diva OR an authentic and modern author with a desire to capture a niche audience...I will let you decide.

You find yourself scrambling for the right word, tone, context, writing style and font yet scrutinizing every word as you imagine the editor of your future publishing company taking his ragged edged teeth torn red pen to your masterpiece. Yet, deep down you, desperately want the red pen to make an appearance because at least that means there is interest.

So, you see, you can purchase the best technology, source the perfect writing location, have the most exciting and interesting content, in your opinion, that a book requires but, if you do not possess inspiration and desire to capture an audience, then you are not doing it right.

It also helps if you your story is not as dull as watching test cricket on a summer's day.

Who actually enjoys that?

This journey has already taken on arms and legs resembling that of a drunken octopus on a Saturday night. It has taken some rather harsh words of reality in the mirror to find a core message and a streamlined story that will not have you either wanting to take a biro to my eye balls (or your own for that matter!) or in actual fact resort to hardcore alcohol just to take away the pain.

I write with the kindest and most authentic intention, but knowing I cannot help my inner sarcastic diva and her inability to rein it in; there might be on occasion, some offence and insult thrown in for good measure.

I trust you will grow a pair, man up, move on or de-friend me on Facebook. The latter being something I will find terribly difficult to cope with and will no doubt require medical treatment to suppress the angst. On the other hand, maybe not.

Speaking of Facebook, it has ironically been pivotal in providing me the platform for my humorous approach to writing. Whether I can convert the rationed 50-word status into a full legible script of wit and emotion is another story, I am fully engorged in the utter denial that this feat is doable. Moreover, doable well. I am, after all, a unicorn chaser with mental issues.

It is unlikely anyone will stop me in my quest to cause my readers to require a change of underwear or at least a tissue to wipe their joy-filled tears.

It really is highly satisfying knowing you have made someone laugh.

Giggle.

Breakdown in hysterics and fall on their face whilst you stand there like Mr. Chuckles instead of helping them. For content purpose, alone you understand.

Causing hysteria, in the mass form; something I will never tire of. It is, in my humble opinion, enriching for the soul.

This is the story of Melanie Arlene Hume and her journey to the desert disco…

Let us start shall we…

Submerged in a vortex or abandoned childhood. The remnants of an abandoned family occupied the house on Crum Crescent, Stirling. A broken and proud man rose from the ashes of his heartache and braved the trek to Borestone Nursery to surgically detach his infant 3-year-old from his ankles. Me. Picture it…

I am clinging to his ankles like the vulnerable and scared child I actually was. Alone, frightened and at 3 years old harboring the fear that my one remaining parent will leave. Moreover, not come back. He did, because I am fabulous, but more about that later. In chapter 2, 3, 4 well pretty much them all! (Insert obligatory LOL here).

I can still smell the air, the surroundings, the petrol leak in his small red van, the feeling of being held in his arms, being led up the path to the Nursery entrance and the Nursery Teacher greeting me with that almost force sense of cheese. She was actually very lovely. Not lovely enough to suppress the tantrum that was about to ensue when he uttered the words "I will come and collect you later darling". Em no. What? Nope, there was no memo received on that point.

Beechwood Park. Ah Beechwood Park. The mere sound of those beautiful words was like crack cocaine for my ears. The promise of a trip to Beechwood Park if I calmed down, stopped having a tantrum that could only be described as the exorcist on a bad day, released the strangling grip from my my dad's neck and relaxed. At 3 years old, the promise of a trip to the Park was heavenly. That and a cone. A "99". Remember them? When they actually were 99 pence. Now a fiver.

And so, dad left. Where he went that morning and how he felt I would never know. I can tell you, I felt lost. I imagine any child feels that way but I only know me. Moreover, I felt lost. Then Ms. Kindergarten Kiki gave me crayons. In fact, I think an actual pen accidentally slipped into the mix and my goodness, all hell broke loose on those walls. It was like a Crayola massacre.

In addition, Milk at 11am. Those were the days it was free. A government initiative that afforded children free milk daily… Long gone. A bit like Kiki's sanity by that point. Bless her. She was never the gem that was Linda Rose Andersen. Our crèche leader. God rest her soul. What a champ.

Dad came to collect me at 1pm. Bouncing in that door like a proud papa bear. Of course, I am like a starved dog and hound him immediately for attention. Because clearly the Crayola gangbang and the free full fat, milk just was not enough to satisfy my needs. So off we trot to Beechwood.

For those that remember the days of Beechwood Park and the rental bikes, I adored that past time. Ashleigh, my older sister, and I used to frequent that and whizz around the bike tracks happy as Larry. Larry is not an actual person. Although I did have an imaginary friend once and he was called Harry. Same thing.

Anyway, at 3 years old it was just the swings that enriched me with joy. Strapped in and off I went, pushed back and forth on the red swings whilst I felt the brisk Scottish wind "skelp" my face like a wet cloth. Sheer bliss. I remember I was wearing red shoes that day and my little lace was coming undone. My dad fixed that. Like he fixed everything. Still does. Except Formula one tickets, that is my sole purpose in adulthood. I missed the memo. Yet again.

Swings and Pizza with Heinz beans and sausages on top were my two favorite things at 3 years old. That and the cuddles from my dad and my big sister, Ashleigh.

Ashleigh, 2 years older in age but at 5 years old my best friend. My only friend. Apart from Harry. Oh and my disco Barbie. She ruled the school. She never talked back though.

I secretly hoped one day she would turn around and say, "For god sake Melanie put some clothes on me". Then I could have been a child prodigy with the talking Barbie. I would of course now be Macaulay Culkining my way to rehab. Lucky escape. Although, cutting the hair of my Barbie's was something I became obsessive over. More on that later.

So yes, my big sister. Hated me half the time. Most of the time probably. Ok all of the time. However, with just big daddy cool flying solo, it was a dog eat dog world in the Hume household. I loved her so. Still do. She is mentally unstable in many ways but she has taught me many things in life. First and foremost, how to act sober, when drunk on 2.99 merry down at 16 years old. She is quite the little rascal.

We spent many nights wondering what was going on in our family. It was all a little dysfunctional yet it worked. My dad had a barrage of support around him offering to babysit. I am uncertain of how these people survived. We were a pair to be reckoned with.

My Aunts; Alexis, Pamela and Wendy, who, like the Witches of East wick, did most things together. Young sisters living the dream. Raising us. Truly blessed to have had them in my childhood.
In addition, they have video evidence to hold me hostage to until my grave!
Dancing and singing up and down the hallway at 5 years old, thinking I was Tina Turner. That video is highly amusing viewing. That was a sure fire sign I was destined for greatness I am certain of it. Not sure about the haircut I was sporting though. I looked like a boy. Until I was about eight. Maybe that is why my Barbie has never talked back…

Many a night was spent at their house. My grannie's house. I wish I could remember her more. Her touch, her smell, her voice. I know she loved us deeply and I know she was and is terribly missed. Her girls did her proud though for the support and encouragement they provided to my dad in his time of need was extraordinary. Moreover, selfless. They are heroes in my eyes.

I remember so many fun times with Pamela, Wendy and Alexis. All individually but also together.

The trip to Blackpool when I was seven. That was epic. Ashleigh went on the Grand National and required sedation and new underwear after. Hilarity ensued whilst I gambled away my small fortune of what can only be described as 4564 1p pieces. Blackpool had such an uplifting holiday vibe and when Alexis and Pamela took us there I loved every minute. I did lose a sparkly wig though. Remember those wigs that these holiday resorts sell at the gift shop. The ones that are bright colored etc. Well this one was like gold tinsel. And some creep stole a hat from a 7-year-old. Again, what is happening in this world when people are stealing other people's wigs? Not that I required a wig, I just liked to stand out. And be Tina Turner. Obviously.

Standing out was my internal sadness crying out for attention. I craved affection. Not because I felt unloved, on the contrary I was loved tremendously; but because my heart was fractured. Thus, feeling submerged in my own sorrow.

2

The early years

Being the younger of two small children in a single parent family undoubtedly had its benefits. Ashleigh and I had my dad wrapped around our fingers. He adored us. He still adores us. He will always adore us.

It takes a dedicated, selfless human being to make the choices he made at such a young age. To define his life by parenthood when the odds were stacked against him is not just admirable, but is heroic. To selflessly suppress and willingly deny yourself the freedom to reach for your dreams and instead create a new dream in raising your two girls to be the women you want them to be; empowered, respectful of themselves and others and compassionate. Like their dad. Their hero, their icon and their idol in life. What compelled a single man to naturally choose this path in life?

I was not an adult then, obviously! However, I have a memory that serves me the joy of remembering times worth cherishing and there were many. There were tough times, and right enough, there were many of them too. I would like to share some of these times with you, for they will no doubt bring a smile to your face, whether you are laughing out of hilarity or with tears of joy. In addition, they shared with the deepest sincerity and poise, and if you know me personally, with the utmost respect for anyone referenced. Granted, if you do not know me personally, I hope you feel you do!

(Dad, disclaimer here is that some of this content will make you cringe!)

Therefore, there I was, 5 years old, sporting a cropped haircut that caused my gender to come into question. Who does that to their child? God bless my dad for choosing an easy route to dress and ship his kids to school each day. Bless him; my pinafore and my Borestone Primary school tie were always pressed to perfection but the hair! The goddamn hair. Even though I was far too young for vanity (or was I?), it was a crucial factor in defining my choices for glamour in later life. More about that in the later years. By that point you will have grasped I am either mentally unstable but a gifted comedian or I am a narcissistic yet loveable storyteller. I am hopeful for both. My money (Abu Dhabi Dirhams to be precise!) is on both. I will prove any sceptics wrong. This tale of autobiographical memoirs is sure to be one you do not want to miss. Alternatively, maybe you do, but humor me.

Now my inner ego had many friends at Primary School. On the other hand, maybe not. It probably was not just the hair. I was sporting a rather large body for a child. Nevertheless, hey, more to love right? Apparently not. However, can I really judge kids of 6-11 for harboring the cruelest tongue and expressing the vilest commentary in my general direction every day or every week or every school year? Until I left.

My 7th birthday. A day I will never forget. What 7-year-old do you know whose father arranges for a meal at the local restaurant, accompanied by my Primary 3 boyfriend, Thomas, who lived directly across from the school? He bought me a My Little Pony jigsaw, chocolates (of which I did not need, but scoffed anyway) and a Barbie. An actual Barbie, from Woolworths. Remember that shop? The first floor of Woolworths in Stirling was home of the Barbie collection. And oh my word, it was heaven shopping there on a Saturday. Any day, every day.

Anyway, back to my date. My dad took Thomas and I to Little Johns, a small family owned restaurant in Stirling. We sat together, unaccompanied and had our dinner. It was so lovely. My dad was in the restaurant, no doubt hidden somewhere discreet loading a shotgun ready to pounce. But in reality was with his good friend Laurence, who was top chef at LittleJohns. Although I was young, that night, I was filled with excitement. Excited to be adored by someone other than my dad.

Adoration, a strong word. Nevertheless, a word I use regularly to describe my childhood. Yes, we did not have much materialistically, but I was adored.

The following day at school, my trip to LittleJohns with Thomas unfortunately sparked some gossip in the playground. Children can be so cruel. Someone spat on me. I do not recall the exact reason why, although I know it was certainly not justified, but I do know people did not like that, I was smiling. I could never understand why someone's sadness breeds excitement and satisfaction in others.

The culprits responsible for this and many other occasions during my early years at Borestone were the cause for my hatred of myself by the time I was nine.

They called me fat, ugly, pregnant, abandoned, crazy, stupid, obese, unloved and hated. Strong and powerful words for a child who has nowhere to turn, but home.

I have chosen not to name anyone related to this particular time of sorrow in my memoirs, not because I am scared or apprehensive about backlash, but because they have no place in my book. A book filled with memories that albeit are tough to recall and record, but also pivotal in shaping my personality and dreams. Those that bred cruelty and hatred are not part of my journey. I forgave them a very long time ago for harboring hatred or resentment for neither nourishing nor pleasant for the soul.

Therefore, for now we will refer to them as Itchy and Scratchy. There were two.

Two children, same age, same class, same town, same gender. Different outlook on human decency, appreciation of human kindness and I truly question if they possessed a heart. I sometimes wonder if karma ever darkened their door.

I feared walking home every day for 5 years. I walked home, in fear every day, making sure I either could see my sister or was close to her. Even though she found me incredibly irritating, she was my hero, my friend and my protector in my dad's absence.

I remember the long walks home, along the Glasgow road, down onto Clark Street, down the lane and up on to Crum Crescent felt like a lifetime. I longed for someone to protect me from cruelty. I was not a strong willed young girl. I just wanted friends. I wanted to be liked. To fit in. I did not though. In their eyes, I was an overweight unfortunate looking girl who did not conform to what was deemed acceptable. This really hurt my feelings. I already harbored a lack of understanding of why my own mother didn't want to be my friend; and now Itchy and Scratchy had turned what felt like the whole school against me. They even took my lunchbox. It was Thomas the Tank. I loved him. He was my friend. I can recall that theme tune any day.

They stopped me one day on my way home from school and pushed me. They pulled my hair and spat on me again. They told me that I was not loved because I was ugly and that is why my mother left. Abandoned us. I believed them. I was frightened. I just covered my head and my face so that at least they could not see my tears. That must have been my innate way of masking my sadness. Either way, it infuriated them even more.

They belittled me in gym class, talked over me in assembly, made up stories about me and spread them around school. Primary school. This was the 80's. I dread to think how bad it must be nowadays.

I took solace in singing, country dancing and reading passages from the bible that Miss McQueen gave me. I used to read them every day after we had our Milk. I like to think that is what gave me faith. I am not, nor was I ever religious, but it gave me courage to believe that a better day would come.

Miss McQueen discovered my singing voice. That was a special day. We were rehearsing for the Burns supper and she asked that I sing Auld Lang Syne.

I stood, in class and belted out that song. And boom, instantly I gained a friend. My teacher.

After school care was a time I really enjoyed. I remember that day my singing was discovered I could not wait to get home and tell my Auntie Wendy. Ashleigh and I would go there after school whilst my dad worked. She used to make the best tuna and onion sandwiches and soup. She was so patient. And so young. But had the innate capability to adopt a maternal approach to our safety and wellbeing. Her, along with Pamela and Alexis; the three sisters; took turns to care for us, their nieces. And in doing so, helped my dad retain some routine, independence and sanity. I know it must have been emotionally daring doing everything alone. All whilst trying to retain some self-respect and dignity. He was always cool though. Like Danny Zukko. Cool as. He was my dad. I loved how cool he was. Everyone loved how cool he was.

My dad was so cool he drove a van that had a name. Danny. White transit van. Danny the tranny. Riding to school was a fun experience. Morning routine was regimented. Get up, get dressed, eat breakfast, get in Danny, go collect Siobhan (my dads' friends' daughter) and then go to school. Siobhan was always late. I remember every single day my dad peeping and telling us to roll down the window so he could shout as loud as he could to Frances (her mum) "is the bairn ready". Which she was not. Not ever. And so finally, she runs out to the van. Now she was a couple of years younger than me but so cute. And we could never understand why her name was spelt silently. It was confusing. Shevonne would have been easier to understand but naw. Si o ban was the best spelling apparently. Not a family to conform clearly. She had long hair. I wanted long hair so a part of me hated her a little. In addition, the uncanny resemblance she had to her mum was unreal. Like mirror image. Frances Cummings, a truly lovely human being. Such a good friend to my dad. And to us. And still is.

And so another Monday morning assembly arrived and at 9 years old, we are all together talking about our weekends and I had told Miss McQueen that I met my dad's bird. The whole class was interested to know what kind of bird. I went onto explain how she was tall, pretty, stayed over and drove a fiesta. Of course, the whole class and Miss McQueen were puzzled as to how a bird can drive a car…

I was of course referring to my dad's new girlfriend, Morag.

She got an eyeful and a mouthful that weekend. I was yet to receive my long awaited birthday gifts; the doll whose hair would grow if you motioned her hand up and down; and the purple unicorn toy from page 465 of the Argos Catalogue. This was to be called Ralph. He would have been my best friend. So there was I, at 8 years old, screaming at the top of my lungs at my dad because I have consumed myself with such impatience that I have failed to clock that my dad has found a bird…

And a smile was born.

I eventually got my doll. I was utterly mesmerized by her hair and the fact it grew out of movement in her arms. Who invents this stuff? I want him to invent me a man who is…

Ahem.

She was my best friend. I called her Sarah. Sarah and I used to go everywhere together. I secretly prayed to Santa that he would bring me the ability to grow my hair from going all Olivia Newton John and getting physical with my arms, as she does in the Xanadu video. Nope, did not work. I did get a Christmas that year I will never forget. We had another person around. It was magical.

The New Year came and went and things started to change around our family. Not my hair, it was still refusing to grow like some adolescent pain in my ass not budging.

I learned to finger knit. That was an achievement in itself! God bless Kate Weston who had the patience of an angel. Not a saint, for a saint she was not. A potty mouth aye. Saint no. Lovely woman though. Her husband friendly with my dad. She taught me to knit. To actually create something from two simple objects and make a masterpiece. I was not quite advanced enough to make a piece of clothing though. More a small throw/knitted cover that could keep a borrower warm. Small but neat. Unlike my body frame.

Then a day came that ignited a feeling in me I have never been able to explain.

The day my dad told us he was marrying Morag. I was so happy because I wanted a mum. And she cuddled me as if I was her own. She rebuilt our faith in maternal kindness and I tucked her love safely in my heart.

I looked at her like a possessed infant desperate for acceptance. I longed for her to marry him, quickly. So that she could not then leave. Not that I needed to. She was not going anywhere. She had parked any self-righteousness she had the day she met my dad. She possessed sheer selflessness that I sometimes wondered if she might be a saint. To suppress her own dreams and plans only to adapt to the dysfunctional single parent existence. Ultimately completing a family with her sheer presence alone.

My dad looked content. I had seen my dad express many emotions in my formative years; some of which were not memories I recall with a heartfelt smile, more sadness, but to see his face fueled by hope was a special time. He was a changed man. A changed father. He exuded restored hope in his eyes and you could see it in his mannerisms. I immediately knew this was a beautiful thing that was happening.

Unfortunately, though, with happy times comes sad times. Around the time they decided to marry Morag's father passed away. I only met him once or twice but if I had the opportunity to meet him again, as an adult this is what I would say to him:

"Sir, I want to thank you. Thank you for raising a beautiful daughter. With a kindness in her soul we have never known. With a selfless and compassionate adoration for other people I am eternally grateful for. She has changed our lives. She has afforded my sister and I the luxury of knowing what it is like to have someone we can call mum. She has not run, objected or shown any signs of discomfort and we are completely in love with the idea that she is joining our family. She is marrying our hero and although we are a little jealous of all the attention she is receiving, she deserves it. I hope to one day make her proud to call me her own, because to me, she is the only mum I will ever know, and she misses you. Every day"

Nevertheless, alas, life does go on and a wedding was planned for June 14 1991.
A glorious day. My hair was still short but by this point Morag, god love that woman, had resurrected a non-masculine hairstyle from the remnants on my younger years and cut a stylish bob, only the early 90's 9 year olds would understand.

So there I was sporting a new bob. Thinking I am the best thing since the sliced bread my mother ran off to buy. The bob rocked my world. I would stroll around, again, thinking I was Tina Turner singing 'Nutbush', rocking my new haircut. Except on this day, we had been sent to the local hairdresser to have a blow dry for the wedding of the year.
Then came the pink puff pastry. I mean bridesmaid dress. Keep reminding yourself this was the 90's. A time for outfits that resemble items from a dessert menu.

It was a grand affair. Notwithstanding the obligatory emotional outburst at the Registry

Office. On my Uncle Douglas' crisp white and unbelievably crease free shirt. I felt immense relief though. For a number of reasons.

Reason number 1. The law deemed it the norm for marriage to presume husband and wife lived together, so she was not leaving! Yaldi.

Reason number 2. She insisted we call her mum. In a non-aggressive, "I really do love you" kind of way.

Reason number 3. I could finally tell all my school friends that I did have a mum and she was a hairdresser who streamlined my gender by fixing my hair. Those short hair school days were tough.

Reason 4, and by far the most important reason was that my dad smiled. He had found contentment and a woman who resurrected his faith in humanity and love.

Nevertheless, back to the fashion in those days. I feel it is deserving of discussion. What was it about the 90's that convinced people into thinking and believing that fashion should be as equally distasteful and outrageous as the many blasphemous adjectives the dresses undoubtedly attracted? Honestly. You should see the pictures. I am not certain if I looked more like a constipated animal or a miserable tiny human at the sheer prospect of sharing my dad with yet another female!

And so the wedding was my most favorite childhood memory. A day we welcomed Mum into our family. She swiftly filled that maternal role with lectures a go-go and the 60p lunch money ready every morning! Remember the days when 60p was more than enough for chips at lunch. Alternatively, for my American readers, "French fries". (She says hopeful that the American readers buy in abundance so that I make the New York Times Bestseller List).

And so we were a family. And with family time came annual trips to Butlins. In Skegness. A truly exciting and beautiful holiday destination filled with the typical unpredictable British weather.

Remember Butlins? When it was the place to be. With the Red Coats here and the Red Coats there, here a coat, there a coat, everywhere a coat coat. The bees' knees! You only needed 20p and that lasted a full day no word of a lie. The days when things, you know "stuff" was cheap and a fiver lasted a whole weekend. But the memories priceless. When you used to have to visit the local Superdrug for a film for your camera. Because digital was a strange word in those days. Taking photos and capturing memories was a risky business until the early noughties. A hit or a miss that you would get anything more than two or three decent photographs from your spool of 24 or 36. And the sheer excitement you had if your film allowed more than the standard quantity. Then the 24 hour "quick" express service offered to develop your spool was just too much to handle. Then the slow escalator approaches up to the first floor in boots with sheer anticipation to collect your photos. Of which it never crossed your mind that the photo staff had a good laugh at your failed attempt at photography for only three of your pictures were in focus. And so, you pay, you leave and you sat in the mall center seats opening your photo pack with baited breath ready to "ooo" and "ohhh" at what can only be described as a vortex of photo failure. But wait, that one pic you did not expect to be good, is outstanding. And so, you are reminded of joy once again. And to celebrate this momentous achievement it was decided that a trip to McDonalds was required. 10 years old and McDonalds was the number one place for calorific fulfilment.

McDonalds Big Mac Meal deal? Remember that. The days of the 2.88 and the bus fare in and out of the town was a Saturday spent at Maccy D's! With most of the youngsters from your school and the notoriously shady "other" school in the district! Of which there were many. Of course, it was the 90's version of speed dating naturally. Go in, eat, chat to random people, make a few friends, and hear of some random wannabe who wants to "pash" on with you! Absolute cringe factor. Like X factor but without the talents. Remember the only way of communications in those days is actual talking to each other. Albeit through a sniggered and coy eye exchange whilst chomping on your delicious fries, at what can only be described as the speed of lightning. The smell alone was so enticing you could sit for hours salivating at the various options available for the same price as your 3-photo creation! Nevertheless, for delinquents alike, it was the place to be. There and Stirling Ice Rink. The epitome of disco light, orange juice filled banter. With what can only be described as Scotland's answer to non-educated delinquents. And of course picking the hardest balancing act to appear alluring and interesting to the opposite sex at such a young age was nothing short of dramatic. And shady. And why was it that there was never a decent pair of skates? Always the ones with "the snapped lace" or the "blood smears from another user". Not to mention that as soon as my feet touched the ice I would rather have been subjected to a beating in the street. The thought of trying to move like a professional and keeping cool at the same time remained my prime priority, but unfortunately, my minds mental deficiency meant it completely unachievable. And taking my friends down with me when I took a nosedive for the ice was probably the sole reason I walked the lonely ice road alone. All the live long day. I fell almost every 17 seconds. I was neither cool nor alluring. So McDonalds was my natural first choice for future inter gender liaisons. And stuffing my face. It is no wonder I had a weight issue. I was eating my feelings.

So, reaching 11 years old and being overweight was becoming quite noticeable in terms of my maturing into a teenager. As referenced before, kids can indeed be cruel and the thought of leaving primary school was relieving. However, the stark reality of moving onto a bigger school, and being the youngest chicks in the farms again had not quite dawned on me. Until the end of the summer. My Primary 7 signature stained school shirt was no longer. The "friends" I had in P7, albeit not always nice, were all I had. In addition, most went to a different high school, so the thought of entering the yard of big bad animals became a real fear in the pits of my stomach. Not because making friends was difficult, goodness, I had already known that and it been a reality for years; it was the fear that I would indeed be immediately exposed for being different. Different in terms of size, background etc. The only caveat to that reality is that I already had an older sister at that school. Remember her? A protector. Or perhaps not.

3

Low school

Worst years of my life. Ages 11 – 16. More sad and destructive memories than good. But the core of my ability to stand up for my own protection and future independence was born.

First year in High School. Reconnecting with my old Primary School friend was my main reason for smiling on day one. She had moved to another district 3 years earlier therefore had seen her late primary years spent in another school. But we went to the same high school and I was filled with sheer excitement at seeing my best friend again. It was somewhat naive of me to think that I would still be considered hers. Of which I was not. That is to be expected. However, certainly not understood at such a young age. Therefore, you can imagine that felt a bit rejected on the first day of high school. I must have been a right joy to be around. Probably did not help in me attracting new friends. Honestly. Should have known better. I did have one friend, Kirsty. She was quite the geek. So as a two-some, we were clearly a force to be reckoned with.

The school, Bannockburn High, was the brightest orange building in the world. It was huge, ghastly colored and sporting some seriously intelligence intolerant individuals. Only a short distance from my house so an easy and terror free walk to and from school. At first.

Having a timetable of different subjects was pleasantly surprising. Learning language in the morning and creative music, the afternoon meant for an enjoyable curriculum but my desire to learn and not be distracted by delinquency surrounding me did not come without critique. Or bad seeds.

I thoroughly enjoyed French. Mr. Seamus Black, the teacher, was a fine human. A very handsome man too. But the French language oozed from his native tongue like a beautiful piece of classical music. I was utterly engrossed in learning and absorbing his experience, his cultural approach to teaching and ultimately wanted to fluently interact in class. I found it liberating to escape Scottish reality and pretend to be French. Such a joy in that department.

Unfortunately, I did not possess such a feeling about Physical Education. It was extremely apparent that my body type, weight, general unhealthy pastime had become reality in this class. The teachers held no mercy either. Being exposed was quite literally the most humiliating experience in my life, but on the plus side, I had THE best handwriting in school and less than desirable kids regularly asked me to write their notes to get out of class. I had a following. A regular following of people needing a fix. I was like their drug. Very amusing. Yet I was still fat. Why could that not just go away and not be a factor in my life. Always churning at the pits of my stomach, literally. Always staring back at me in the mirror and in gym class. Every single lesson. Hated myself. Even in the mid 90's it was never cool to be fat. I ate my feelings regularly and it is any surprise I did not start eating people like Hannibal. Boys more than girls would regularly ask if I was pregnant. One time my teacher laughed. I will never forget that or her outrageous hair. She resembled a raccoon. I took solace in that. At her age, her looks would never change but I might one day turn into a supermodel. Unlikely but whom are you to judge an 11-year-old. Hilarious.

Therefore, first year was a long, unfriendly, lonely and exhausting experience. Meeting new people, of whom some would become enemies, acquaintances or lifelong friends. Lifelong friends becoming something I can count on one hand as this book is written in my later years. Twenty years since I went to high school. Saying that aloud has sparked yet another grey hair. What is it with grey hairs that poke their nose into your 30's like an obsessed mother? First year in High School introduced me to many things; the most memorable, and not for the right reasons, was a group of people I longed to forget in a hurry upon leaving school.

I did meet one girl. Michelle O'Neill. Nice girl. Tall, attractive, stylish. I thought, yes I should befriend her. She was sporting a questionable fringe but that was all the rage in those days. Remember this is the early 90's. Saved by the Bell, Heartbreak High and Sweet Valley High consumed your Saturday mornings! Befriending her though, that did not come without struggle and the obligatory glance of distain from her friends. Friends she had grown with through primary. Nevertheless, surprisingly I integrated quietly into that well establishes group. A desire to mingle with boys and merry down cider on a weekend meant you fitted in well. Too well. I used to daydream in class. Learning about make-up, boys, fashion, education, empties, carry outs, slang terms for all things your parents would of course ground you for, but knew they had done the exact same thing.

I accepted an invitation to join a "friend" one evening, a Tuesday evening. I remember it very well as Heartbreak high was on BBC2 at 6.25pm. She asked if I wanted to join her and some others at the "Tole", a local shopping precinct frequented by gamblers, teens and the like. A horrific night of fear, anxiety, bullying and ultimately long-term damage ensued. An older girl from the rival school (I use rival loosely) approached me as I stood minding my business. Having never seen this girl in my life I do what any normal human does and said hello.

Slap.

She took a full force shot at my right cheek. Wow. The pain was unbearable. Nevertheless, the shock meant I stood for about 20 minutes, or so it felt, in awe of what had just happened. All I could think was why. Her sad and pathetic reasoning was that she did not like the look of me. I was 12 years old. She was 16. The "friends" that had clearly invited me as a ruse were now no-where to be seen. Alone and scared I took solace and refuge in a local fish and chip shop. They could see I was scared and vulnerable. Boy, I was scared. They called my home and I spoke to my dad who came to collect me. I do not think I have ever encountered fear like that. To not know what prompted someone to be so vicious and physical with her rage consumed my mind for quite some time after.

The next day at school was interesting. Apparently, news of my assault was something of a joke. Very funny. I chuckled along with everyone. Did I hell. I could feel my mind wandering into a dark deepened hole of sadness. Why did she do it? And how did it manage to make school headlines in a matter of 12 hours. She did not go to my school but my unfortunate experience had reached the playground of my school and my sadness was big news. Big news indeed. I often likened that feeling to a feeling of grief. Grief stricken at the departure of the remaining fragments of my self-respect and dignity. To know the true meaning of that loss at age 12 was compounding. Her bitter act of hatred had left me fragile and fractured. No one and nothing could eliminate the nightmares that followed for around 2 weeks after. Scared to walk to school, scared to walk home, scared to even answer the phone. However, I studied hard. At 12 years old, I loved my French class. And eating. Lord, I loved eating.

Why didn't people like me? I did not understand why.

Speaking of eating. For a 12-year-old I was packing a mean shell. Clearly was not a poverty stricken starved infant that I am certain of. But I had a fondness for portions made for armies. Where do appetites like that come from I wonder? On occasion, I would have happily eaten a person. I think that was illegal, and mentally unstable. Still is. Oh well. Not that eating was my main ambition in life you understand. That was making friends. I longed for someone to like me. I just was not cool. Neither was half my school right enough so theory taught me to aim for the non-cools. So I did.

In addition, allowed my mum to continue perming my hair. Resembling a farm animal post electrocution, that hairstyle was "all the rage". Everyone sported curls only an afro comb could handle. And mousse. Everyone used at least two cans of mousse a minute. To get those curls living the Beyoncé life was a regimented process involving sculpture skills only the finest artists possessed. So, at least my hair was something of a fashion statement, even if my body type and cool effect were less than desired in terms of what was "too cool for school".

Black eyeliner. That was another fashion must. I was convinced that black eyeliner and my outrageous perm were my gateway into hanging out with the cool kids. Both after school and at weekends.

I had only turned 13 when I started to notice that some of the cool kids actually embraced my presence. Well, as far as one 13-year-old can actually embrace another 13 year olds presence. I might be writing rather enthusiastically there. Most weekend gatherings involved frequenting near to the entrance of the local ethnic minority supermarket often called by a name that is outrageously racist. But people knew.

There wasn't anything of great interest to do there but frequenting there and then moving a mere 2 meters' circumference for the entire evening was considered a wild night out. Fortunately, the local Chinese takeaway a mere five meters away often enticed us to purchase something from their delicious menu; fried rice. Alternatively, chips. Not forgetting the fork. Indigestion ensued. Then we always seem to have an abundance of merry down silver label masquerading as a bottle of diet coke. In a bottle that had been resurrected more times than you have seen a hot dinner. And let us face it you have had many of those. So there we all were, slowly reaching intoxication in the dark on a cold winter's night, with our cheap cider, bought by the equally unwilling 18-year-old delinquent desperate to cling on to his youth. But, if you had fried rice or chips surely the stench of booze or the incapability of acting sober would disappear. Em no. I could not blend in when intoxicated. Partly because I was a rather obese 13-year-old at this point. Not to mention a teenager with a penchant for cheap booze. It was affordable and within the pocket money budget, though so it was of course legal and perfectly ok. Occasionally we would upgrade to Thunderbird if we had a spare "pound". Thunderbird was a tonic wine. Utterly horrific but you felt liberated if you still had enough buck in the bank to afford that instead of the merry down. Thunderbirds are a go go. So was the hangover! To get one over your parents' utter lack of knowledge as to how bolstered you are being up there with achievements of the 90's. That and passing my exams. More on that later.

So there was this one night. Never forget it. Bloody cold so it was. Hanging out at the Park in Hill park with the copious bottles of pocket money juice and I decide to pay my biological mother a visit…

My mother. A sharp woman, who had been very inactive in my life to that date, lived a mere one mile from my house. And less from the park. So the bold Melanie decides right I am going to go ask her why she abandoned my dad, my sister and me when I was two. I mean, she will welcome me in with open arms surely. No. She was hosting a dinner party. I laughed. Chapped the door, no answer. Chapped again. Her husband answers. AWKWARD.

"Hiya, is Shirley in"

"Ehhhhh"

"Aye Pal, let me get her for you"

"Great"

(She comes to the door)

"Hi, I am drunk"

So I am standing facing my mother. I am having an "ongoing crises", you know the type of crisis life reserves for you at the grand old age of 50 and yet here I am having an emotional meltdown and I am barely a teenager. She was a woman who I had not touched, smelled, hugged, embraced or even spoken to in 11 years. The impact that significant moment had on my drunken state was unbelievable. I was sober in around 37 seconds. By god, I resembled her. Still do. I think I must have stood and stared at her for an age. I remember she offered me water. And obviously invited me into the kitchen. Not the living room where her dinner party guests were trying to not look too curious as to whom the random 13-year sizeable teenager resembling the modern day Oliver was. Therefore, I was ushered into the kitchen. And I am trying to compose my drunken state. Whilst trying to avoid contact with every human in a 100-mile radius. Hilarious. I then burst into tears. I could not quite figure if I was in shock, scared for my impending lecture if I arrived home intoxicated or was just utterly miserable at having guzzled a full liter of utter garbage. Perhaps all three. It was however, a short-lived visit and I began my journey home. Home to a house of love. But perhaps not on that night seeing as I was 50 shades of miraculous.

Now, I should probably mention that it was a sleet ridden, snow infested cold winters blistery winded night in Scotland. In addition, the Bannockburn road that connected her house to my house had unfortunately not escaped the realms of risky pathways because of said weather conditions. Therefore, you can imagine my sheer delight when I took a dive into said pathway and very quickly looked like I had soiled myself. Which I might have done but my mind was not intact with the movements of my body. I was convinced neither could be determined from my body language though. WOW. How wrong was I?

And so, grounded for 1 month. To a 13-year-old this is soul destroying. I dread to think how delinquents cope nowadays with social media whoring it up in everyone's faces 24/7. There was me, absconded to my shared bedroom. What an utter shit show that was. And not just that day but occupying my mind with "tidying", the obsessive need to be neat and controlling of my tiny environment was undoubtedly me clinging to the only level headedness I possessed at that age.

Picture it, the double bedroom in a two-bedroom terraced house. Split by an upholstered partition, which randomly provided independence to two young girls who hated each other with a passion. On one side was perpendicular city (me!) with everything at the right angle, in place, nothing untoward, bed made, clothes pressed and in wardrobe and an air freshener bringing joy to the world. On the other side, utter carnage. Granted she had the side with no window light but my god was it the complete opposite. And so, we were ruled completely different. Who would have thought it? Two sisters who just happen to have different personalities. And I took mine from Mary not so Poppins. (The mother!). It is funny to reminisce about being 13 years old and already possessing the relevant criteria for diagnosis of a complete neurotic. Utterly neurotic to the core. Regimented daily routine;

make bed, shower, mousse the frizz, diffuse, breakfast, school money and off I went to Prison camp. I mean School. Secondary school of wonders. Or not.

Ashleigh, on the other hand possessed something of a cooler more laid-back nature. Able to just roll with the punches and give zero effort to strolling out the door in the morning. What is that? Was she medicated? Geez some. She had no natural sun light on her side of the room BUT possessed an acceptance of leaving everything at her arse. And it never bothered her. Bothered me. Fuck, it bothered me no end. I am sure I developed a twitch. She would have that bloody bed lamp on until yon time reading and reading and reading some more. Certain she was trying to condemn me to utter aggression.

So another Monday beckons and talk of the classroom is undoubtedly the weekend antics that revolved around the alcohol. And the after parties. Must have been some parties at age 13. Everyone raved about his or her weekends. Some had been camping, shopping, golfing, swimming, ice-skating and the like. Nope, not us. We got utterly shit-faced and collapsed in the snow. Deep joy. Great memories. Of vomit and slurred words. And the obligatory friend who had fallen victim to a shaved eyebrow. That was the punishment in the nineties if you fell asleep at a teenage fueled after party. And boy, it was a shaved eyebrow indeed. Not even a sniff of a hair left on your eyebrow. Gone, to the promise land, never to be seen again. A bit like your dignity, having to walk to school with one eyebrow, if you had not plucked up the courage to even it out and shave the other. Because neither option was pleasing. On the soul or the eyes. However, both were guaranteed to get you attention either way at school, in the playground, at the park, on your way to and from school and probably in your sleep. Sheer hilarity. Never fall asleep at a party. You still went though. You just had to possess the capability of outliving everyone else in terms of your alertness. It was like survival of the fittest. The prize being you got to keep your facial hair. And any self-respect you still possessed even though you already lost a little when you succumbed to the Friday ritual of fried rice and merry down cider.

Mondays usually involved a double lesson of some subject you utterly loathed. For me, it was P.E. Or Physical Education. But sometimes Math's. Whoever enjoyed Pythagoras? In fact, who can tell me they have regularly used those theories in their adult life? Oh yes, I use "that looks like an obtuse triangle" said no one ever. Or discussions of the US Civil War. Unless you are a historian. Again, who does that and remains alert? Wows. I did always enjoy using the word obtuse randomly though. I did eventually grow to enjoy my double lessons though. As I was categorized as a credit level student. The grading system used to determine your level of entry into your standard grade (years 3 and 4 of high school) deemed me the top dollar. Or so I thought. Still do. Credit my ass. Hard work. Nevertheless, I had a penchant for spelling and writing essays so English naturally became my favorite subject. But boy, my teacher was an old witch.

Mrs. Thompson. Highly unapproachable, harsh, rude and Head of the English Department of course. Honestly, entering her class was like walking into the arms of hell itself. She was THE greatest teacher of literature, writing, understanding emotion through words, speaking and interpretation. She was encouraging whilst teaching. It was as if she was in a world of her own oozing self-fulfilling prophecies and endearing us to learn more. But as soon as that bell went, so did the effects of her medication. Gone, never to darken the English department corridor again. And the false sense of security we had been lured into was on its way out. Brave was the student who walked into her class unprepared.

Mrs. Thompson. She taught me the art of making a story flow. And interesting. Keeping the reader entertained but endeared without the worry of falling asleep and ending their day with one eyebrow.

How am I doing?

At age 14, she had me hooked on reading, writing, learning styles of interpretation and poetry. It did not come naturally to me and I did have to work at it, but I took enjoyment from it and found myself possessing some of her "spaced out" qualities when in class. It was liberating to escape into Macbeth, The Merchant of Venice or Romeo and Juliet at least once every day. I often imagined what it would be like to have lived in the Shakespearean era. Gwyneth Paltrow style. Only for the Joseph Fiennes lookalikes, you understand.

I hope you are enjoying the journey so far…

4

The emancipation of sanity

Reaching my 3rd year of High School had taken two whole years of discovery. Albeit mostly unenjoyable for a number of reasons already explained, learning had become solitude for me. I became a slight geek. I enjoyed studying. If I was studying, it was in a quiet place where nothing and no one could interrupt my Zen. Or bully me for want of a better word. Because it never really mattered what I said, done or implied, I always attracted vicious sarcasm or bad feeling.

I chose to learn the language of love; Italian. CIAO BELLA! Mrs. Cathcart. God rest her soul. What a beautiful woman she was. So welcoming and loved teaching. Had the most outrageous hair you have ever seen on a human. Imagine a human poodle. How she acquired said hair is unknown but by god was it outrageous. She spoke French, German and Italian very well though. And taught these languages with such eloquence, her hair was just along for the ride. No judgment here. She was part of a group of equally brilliant teachers. Mr. Black (previously acknowledged due to his epic qualities), Miss Rice and Miss 'Language Teacher'.

Miss 'Language Teacher'. A rather unfortunate soul. Kids were so cruel to her. I was one of them. She had a rather unusual shape, which exaggerated her sizeable derriere. Again, kids were cruel. She took it like a boss though. She knew she was a bad-ass teacher. I eventually stopped joining in. I started to empathize that being a victim of verbal abuse did not warrant me relaying it onto others to regain some self-satisfaction. I could see the sorrow in her eyes. She did have a squeaky voice though. That was irritating as hell. A bit like the times when Ashleigh would keep her light on until the early hours whilst I was trying to sleep on the other side of the room in darkness. But no, she had to read 435 pages before lights out. Cow. Irritating as hell. But, 'Language Teacher', like the others, was a delightful teacher and I loved learning all about the foods and their meanings in French from her. Oh the irony.

Learning language aged me. In a soulful and mature way. I was growing up with interests other than weekend antics involving Chinese food and cheap cider. At the grand old age of 14, I decided I wanted to become a hairdresser. Random choice of profession. However, I wanted a part time job and my own money. I desired to be a girl with her sights high and her head screwed on. However, I chose a vocation that might not pay well and I might not possess the required skills to even be considered talented. And so, I replied to an advert in the Stirling Observer. The local paper that we all scoured every Wednesday for cinema listings, classifieds, information of our school football teams' recent performance and that of every other school in the region. Like a newsletter of current affairs that managed to pull off the cool effect.

"Wanted, Saturday junior; BOOM! I was enticed. The bold I called them. In those days, there was no other means to communicate than actually talking. Gosh, I miss that sentiment with it being so rare these days. So, I am calling and asking if they still require someone and that I have every intention of going to Hairdressing College. Relishing the thought that I would earn my own money, I entered the vortex world of sweeping floors, cleaning towels and making cups of tea. Landed the job. Not that I think there was an inordinate amount of applicants but I like to believe it was because I was charming. And could sweep like shit of a stick. I was to earn 20 GBP a day. For 9 hours of work, 8am to 5pm every Saturday. Never to see a long lie on a weekend day again, except Sundays. Boy, did I exude utter joy at landing this chance at freedom from saving for 27 weeks for a new top. My first shift being the most labor-intensive work I had done to date. Constantly on the go from 8am with "Mel can you wash Mrs. Jones, Mel can you get Mrs. Smith a cup of tea". My twenty bucks was earned. And earned well. I remember the owners were there too, grafting with everyone else. But it was the Receptionist who I liked the most. She was always so lovely to me. And I loved the smell of the salon. The washed hair smell, the sound of the hairdryers going and the seriously strong odor of well hair color filled the salon walls like a fart. Loud and proud. I loved my days there. I used to eat the iced ring biscuits every chance I got. Fold one towel, eat a biscuit. No wonder I was a fatty. Jesus. They stocked them in abundance and I ate my way to a happy disposition by about 11am each Saturday.

Then Barbara would come in for her shampoo and blow dry.

Barbara, imagine it, a Hyacinth Bucket type of woman who just oozed class and richness.

In personality alone. Not to mention she always tipped me two GBP. That was a big deal. Upon hearing her enter the salon, I would without a doubt race to the entrance to ensure I got the chance to wash her hair and get my tip. It never dawned on me that no one else was actually in any hurry to replace me. What a fanny bangle. However, she got exceptional service from Melanie. I think she took pity on me but I did not care. I was all over her like a tramp on a poke of chips. Finishing her hair wash like a boss, I was preparing her for some pampering so I felt like I had contributed to her smile. That was good enough for me.

A few months passed working endless Saturdays and sporting new handbags and shoes because of course I spent as fast as I was earning. The concept of saving was like asking me to not eat. Blew. My. Skull.

"Mel, can we chat to you", came the bold owner's son. I thought shit. They know I eat all the biscuits. Cannot help it. I do go for all the lunches so surely that cancels out *fatty mcfatterson* eating all the iced rings. Phew, it was not the biscuit scandal they wanted to address. No sir. They wanted to discuss my future as a hairdresser. Involving leaving school at the end of 4th year, attending college, earning less than 100 GBP per week for what seemed like 27 years until I was deemed good enough to command more. Sold. Money or no money, I was in awe of them thinking so highly of me. Or did they. I did not care; I was drugged up on the idea that I would one day be the next Vidal Sassoon. Nothing cuter than a naive 14-year-old is there? Yes? No?

Apparently not to Father Hume. All fury broke free from those loveable folks at home. "Melanie, you are not leaving school to become a hairdresser. You will never earn good money". Why does everything boil down to money in life? That was the question in my mind on that day. Why could they not see I was going to become successful with my Edward Scissorhands? Because they were right. Bloody right so they were. You pay bills and then you die was the inevitable meaning of their lecture. Get your highers they would say, go to university they would say. And they were right. However, I was tempted nonetheless to go to hairdressing college. For my step mum Morag was a fine hairdresser and I thought to myself, I would like to be like her. Except, my profession would unfortunately not be my avenue to replicating her fine personality. I would be expected to investigate other routes to that achievement. And more on that later.

I did not understand why they were standing in the way of my dreams. For at that time my dreams had become what the salon had injected me with. Hope, aspirations of becoming something. And my parents were being cruel. Not allowing me to follow that path. For it was surely out of spite. No, it was not. But I believed it at that time. I became resentful.

Resent. A horrible emotion that befalls every human. For a number of reasons. I wanted to really piss off my folks. How dare they stand in the way of my new ambition in life? I shall throw an "empty" and rejoice with my drinking crew. That was my mantra. And boy did it go horribly wrong.

So you see, my dad, a truly brilliant man of course, was a smart motherfucker. Installed a video camera coincidentally at the entrance to the front door of the house and set it to record. Unknown to me.

I had spent the whole week resenting them. And knowing they were to go out for the night on the Saturday of that week I decided to invite all my acquaintances around. I can honestly say it was not solely to spite them, as much as it wanted to show off or appear to be "cool" to these people. Having an open house where scandal would no doubt ensue was seen as a credible and aspirational thing to offer to a group of shady teenagers.

So, off the parents went to enjoy their night. The troops arrived.

The camera is on and recording and I am completely oblivious to this.

All hell breaks loose, things break, these utter morons ruin the simple and angelic lounge of my parents' house and I am in awe of them for at 14 years' old all I want is to be liked. Sad but true.

And so the parents returned. To find me sitting in front of the recording device having discovered that sneaky bastard had pressed record, and I am frantically trying to uncover the "delete all data" button. But no. They stroll in with sheer satisfaction written across their faces at busting me and my disobedient, but desperate antics. And they made me watch it as well. I resembled a scorned pup having been found after a long day of being left alone in the middle of 100 torn pillows, sofa upholstery and curtains. Tail between my legs. Looking at them with a "nothing to see here" expression.

Grounded once again. This was becoming a habit. And I was certain I was now ripping my parents knitting. So to speak. Royally pissing on their harmonious rainbow. Being a rebel if you will. And losing their patience was probably their least favorite thing. I would eventually grow out of that destructive habit but unfortunately, it took a traumatic event to steer my mind into the depths of sorrow and self-hatred. This event being when I experienced real vulnerability with my first sexual experience. At such a young age, it was poignant and disgusting to the core. A traumatic experience I have decided not to explore here and dampen the sheer joy that is my book.

The months that followed were miserable.

I hated everything about myself. My body, my mind, my surroundings. The "friends" that had surrounded me were not a shining example of support in any way. I harbored fear, resentment for my own stupidity, loneliness, vulnerability, more fear and then some additional fear on top of that. Fear that I had allowed myself into a situation that I could never erase. Innocence had escaped me and I was fueled with a mixture of emotions. Hatred, self-loathing, guilt, anger and humiliation. Above all else, shame.

The summer holidays arrived after what felt like years of waiting to escape the sheer hell of school and the suffocation of those spring months that left me feeling submerged in an underwater cage banging on the door hoping, just hoping, that someone would notice my pain. That day never came. What did come were horrible rumors destroying what was left of my dignity. Utterly humiliated at age 14.

However, a new year arrived. School year 4. And with that came Exams. Bloody exams. About as welcome as genital warts. But "paving the way for your future Miss. Hume". Aye well, had the parentals allowed me to advance straight to college, passing go and Old Kent Road, I wouldn't be all that fussed. But alas, I acquired the "must study mantra". And study I did.

Now the sadness I harbored for the workload cast upon us as standard grade students, reminded me of my 9th birthday, receiving a Ken Barbie doll and losing it a mere 6 days later. I mean how does that even happen. I swear one of Morag's clients stole it. I last remember having it in her house in Braco whilst my mum did her shampoo and set. Gone. Bye Ken. Never to be seen again. He was wearing his tuxedo too. What a way to go. RIP Ken, we had a bond. And he had a million-dollar smile. Such a smooth operator. Gone, to the elderly woman in the pink rollers. Boom. Barbie was a now a widower.

And so my Barbie's were unmarried women once again. They never did make Mattel

Barbie cats. At least I did not have access to them. My Barbie's would have had 16 cats,

similar to my aim in adult life. Almost in a salute to feminism and a two finger salute to

men. Or Ken Barbie who buggered off wearing their tuxedo. However, they did have

Barbie jeeps, kitchens and tents. So could at least live comfortably, drive with style and

sleep in the great outdoors on occasion. Groomed to perfection.

And so 4th year was in full swing. It was a long 1st semester back. With standard grade

prelim examinations looming over everyone.

There had been a distinct shift in attention coming my way. Of the ridicule nature. I

seemed to just blend in now and kept myself to myself. Rather introverted if you may. This

solitude contributed to the private rehabilitation my mind so desperately required.

On a positive note, a friends' mum had insisted that her daughter and her friends join her

the following summer at her caravan in the North of England. I had to get approval and

then the countdown would commence.

Countdown commenced as did exams. I slowly began to realizing that my ambitions

extended past the realms of hairdressing and local college. No disrespect but I started to

feel like I owed my dad for his sacrifices and should aim for the best education our fine

government would subsidize. I decided I wanted to become a lawyer; a business law expert

with a view to working in a corporate field. This was going to require real effort and

exceptionally good grades. In a wide range of subjects; arts, sciences, mathematics etc. I

developed this compulsion and competitive streak to beat anyone and everyone on any

preliminary credit test for the next few months. All in preparation for my 4th year exams.

It was a real oxymoron and the epitome of irony that my desperation to leave Bannockburn

High and escape the sorrow that had befallen me. Surprisingly my desire to pass all my exams and receive a free and encouraged pass to Higher Education was more enticing.

However, the summer caravan park 2-week debauchery was about to begin. Only once all eight practical SQA Standard Grade bad boys had pissed all over my rainbow and dented my Zen.

Finally, all practical exams were complete. English, Math's, Office & Information Studies, Chemistry, History, Music, Italian and French. A beautiful collection of learning and nerve-wracking practical's.
There would be a summer long wait for the results, which would seal my fate for future earnings. Was I or was I not a complete moron in terms of my own self-awareness. Or was I actually a credit student after all?

My singing practical was the one I enjoyed the most. I took great joy in learning the art of singing from an actual singing teacher. Mrs. Abram. She knew a vowel or five. "Open your mouth wide Melanie", "sing from your stomach and core Melanie". I was convinced I resembled some fat kid chewing every time a note came from my very mouth. Nevertheless, I was good. I relished in the enjoyment of musical ensemble singing. And any solo piece I was given. I mastered the art of Maria from West Side Story as the sunshine masters the sky. I had the accent perfected and ironically sung, "I feel pretty" like I meant it. Knowing I was actually good injected my confidence and a star was born. In the classroom at least. I scored well that day, I was sure of it. It is a real pity the same could not be said about my Chemistry exam. Atoms just did not cut it for me. Ever. And neither did the periodic table. What is the actual point in the periodic table? How did knowing Mg, the periodic symbol for Magnesium ever fund a mortgage payment? Answer that Einstein will you.

And so my excitement at going away for two whole weeks to a caravan park, with only one parent ratio to five teenage girls, was at a peak. We could barely sleep. Myself and my friends. Friends who were actually friends who cared. I believed that anyway.

The train journey was only about 2 hours but the discussions that took place were not for the faint hearted or those in alcoholics anonymous. For we planned to live like queens and blah our way into buying bottles of Smirnoff like they were maltesers. Easy.

The first night in what can only be described as a rip off Butlins was eye opening. We danced the Macarena. It was 1997 after all. The year of Spice Girls. Wannabe. I was certainly conforming to the lyrics of that song.

I was nominated by the other teenage Spice Girl wannabes to be the one that attempted the 18-year-old stroll to the local supermarket for the Vodka. Boom, sold to the girl with the shady eyebrows (me!) and her wicked dress sense. It was a fun night of discovery, slight debauchery, giggles, boy chat, adult impersonations and chatting to DJ Godar. How I remember his name is beyond me for he was not a handsome sausage. Although he was about 20 years old and looked it. A lot older than us but as he was the DJ, naturally we all wanted to talk to him after the "disco". It is highly amusing that a caravan park has essentially everything you need in a holiday. Access to a beach, food, pool, sports, arcade where you can squander all your money and an accessible village where you can venture out and pretend you are a local or indeed normal. We did it all within the first 24 hours.

For the two-week stint, my parents promised that I could have funds that would last me. So they planned to deposit my bank account at the start of week 2 so spending and budgeting was key. And the good times indeed flowed.

Day 6. Picture it. We are all used to the laws of the caravan land by this point and ruling the school like bosses. More like Spice Girl rejects. However, the Garden Cafe had a member of staff whom decided to chat to me. Out of my five friends, he chatted to me. His name was Phillip. What a beautiful creature he was. A local lad, 16, working part time at the Garden Cafe. Well-mannered, respectable, and enjoyed chatting to me. Me. He actually enjoyed my company. Moreover, I thoroughly fell completely for that sweet romantic. For the remaining days of the holiday, he would join us after his shift, wherever we might be. I was smitten and did not want the holiday to end. I do not think I had ever felt so excited in all my life. It had only taken me 15 years to look at someone in a way that makes your heart skip two beats. The first to remind your body it is real. And the second to reassure my mind that it was real. It was not that he was into my friends and they just were not interested. He was all about Mel. Or "Melz" as many people seemed to call me. It stuck. And I felt cool that I had acquired somewhat of a nickname! I often daydreamed that our care for one another was similar to that of a Take That love song. But realistically how can it at that age? I mean honestly, what 15-year-old is ready to enter into matrimonial harmony? Who wants to be sacrificing the joys of dating in your 20's for wedded bliss and the monthly sky television bill! The X factor is only on TV on a Saturday people.

And so, the holiday ended. A thoroughly enjoyable 2 weeks of discovery. Had my eyebrows waxed for the first time as well. What an eye opening experience that was. Certain the nerves in my eyeballs twitched for a week afterwards at having their virginity ripped from them in a sweeping motion across my face. I swear it was carried out military style. However, an arch was born.

Unfortunately said arched eyebrow was short lived for the follow up at the local beauticians was a bit of a disaster. Why was I landed with the new girl? God bless her. She dropped the waxing stick but accidentally had wax on her uniform and said uniform was accidentally stuck to my eye and she bent down to pick the wax stick up. Took my eyebrow and any remnants of dignity I had left, with her. I looked like a strange albino style scot. Bald eyes.

My love for eyebrows pencils was born. At 16 years old.

5

Talk the talk

16 years old and talking had become my favorite thing! Blagging my way into a job with a

new retailer opening in Stirling had become somewhat of a boss move. Landing the role as

receptionist because I could type fast was a fluke if ever there was one! But I embraced it.

The people of Stirling welcomed their discount superstore of wonders with open arms.

This is 1998 of course. A time of lip liner, over indulged hairstyles and Spice girls fashion

in full force. So platform trainers were a thing of the present. But I had lacked the gift of

style. God love me for trying though. My quest to be the brunette version of ginger spice

was a failed attempt before it had even started! The two blonde streaks that I forced my

mum to inject down the front of my hair to complement the boxed red dye was indeed a

treat for the human eye. Not.

Remember the Union Jack Dress Geri Halliwell wore at the 1998 Brit Awards. That. That was the epitome of style in my eyes. She embodied feminism and sex appeal. Even though looking back I would not have rocked that half as good as she did. She was mental. Ok, she was more than mental but I was inspired by her confidence and wanted to be just like her.

Then I managed to bag myself a part time gig in Miss Selfridge, Thursday shift only but still the best shop in town for girls1 and 25% discount. Holler!

I remember my first shift well. I wore a blue shirt, black trousers, styled my vibrant, Spice Girls reject hair do to perfection, and wore so much make up it weighed my head down! They were the days. I did NOT look like Ginger Spice, more Messy Spice. Still a spice though kens!

Miss Selfridge stockroom was unfortunately about a 20-minute walk from the actual shop floor. Ok, exaggeration, BUT, when people asked for a size not on display or to try on a shoe, I wanted them to die quickly. Or at the very least for center security to play the fire alarm and pronto. I clearly did not understand the concept of customer service at 16 years old. Even with my iced biscuits fueled hairdressing shifts only a few years earlier. Nope, customers, in my eyes, were a bloody hindrance to my daily harmony. On my 4-hour Thursday, shift.

I loved, loved, and loved the plastic carrier bags Miss Selfridge issued with purchases. There was something to be said about the status you felt when purchasing something out of Miss Selfridge or a shop of equal or greater status. Or just asking for a bag like I did. Confidence had possessed me like a poltergeist.

It was a real shame that the same could not be said for the Assistant Manager of that store. She was a real misunderstood woman. Oozed false identity syndrome and screamed insecurity. I felt for her when she used to take calls from her psycho husband/boyfriend, of which I was not sure who it was, every day, at least 5 times. Then barked at us as if it was our fault she had to endure an argument with him. I befriended the full time member of staff, Yvonne, lovely girl. Ran that shop well so she did. She was wasted in retail though. So nice, friendly and approachable and a for a 16-year-old part timer, I felt as if she cared about what I had to say, instead of just barking orders at me. Which the Assistant Manager did all the time. But the pay was good.

It wasn't long though before I discovered that working for Miss S. was sure to secure me an equally good deal a few retailers to the right; USC. The epitome of trend central. And where everyone, who was anyone, bought his or her Timberland boots or Rockport bad boys. Guaranteed to crease your bank account BUT move you a few places up the "cool" chart to trends Ville. And the discount, shit the bed, the discount! There were tiers. Who has tiers! Tier 1, staff discount 30%; Tier 2, Uniform discount, 60%. If you wore it to work, you paid a pittance for it. Result. Imagine the Christmas sales. SHIT THE ACTUAL BED! I was beside myself even though the shifts were long ass and tiring and no Christmas shopper appreciates anything retail staff says or does. And hiring temps who know nothing about anything is a shame on them.

Wearing Timberland moccasins though was my absolute favorite thing. Acquiring Lacoste trainers with my first pay packet was much more important than anything else was. I went nuts. With what was only around 150 pounds, I bought a lot and never looked back.

At 16, I felt accomplished. Like the Wolf of Wall Street. Still an insecure little sausage with deep resentment for all the crazy bitches at my school, but in my personal weekend/Thursday nightlife I was a boss. Working part time at the best retailers in the Marches. The Thistle Marches. The best shopping center in town. The only shopping center in town!

Made some new friends.

Actually made some new friends. FRIENDS. Actual people who had more than a collective one brain cell AND the ability to understand the values and meaning of respecting others. Christ on a bike, it had only taken me 4 years of high school!

Then society introduced mobile phones for the millennium massive. My goodness, everyone had one. Old balk brick style phones from Carphone Warehouse were all the rage and in fashion. So of course, I needed to invest in such a cool accessory if I was to retain my Spice Girl image. Imagine how immediately cool I would look strolling the mall with my empty plastic bag and a brick permanently stuck to my ear. Texts were 10p. Calling anyone was a fortune but the art of calling someone's house to chat to him or her became somewhat unusual. A change was coming. For me, the first thing in desperate need of change to complement my new earpiece was a new haircut.

1998, the year of the Beckhams becoming a household name, not even married yet but dating and it was a popular time for the Spice Girls. Victoria Adams, Posh Spice, had cut all her hair short. So of course, it was only natural that I, a naturally curly head, would choose THE hardest style to manage and go forth to the local Marches hairdresser and ask for "the Posh". Razors were used to skim my neck. Shit you not, I felt liberated and bald at the same time. However, for the first, few days following that cut I regretted it, as I could not for the life of me style it to sit. Forgetting that my hair was naturally curly, GHD's were not even born into society yet AND I lost patience very quickly every single morning. I desperately wanted to be one of those dolls again, you know the dolls whose hair grows upon moving their arms up and down. Why hadn't medical science invented that? Honestly.

A walking talking spice reject was how I felt. But, then one day, through the master of Babyliss straighteners and the school photographer, a selfie diva was born. The pictures were fabulous! Well, perhaps fabulous is a strong word and I should calm this excitement right down to crazy, BUT, it sat well on THAT day. That day where all students in my year were to have the 5th year pictures taken for the school yearbook. My hair was braw. Awesome. Styled. I was THE sixth spice girl and I knew it.

With my new hairstyle came a shift in my outlook. Social circle. Weekend commitments. Outlook on my studies and my shift in how I wanted to enter adult hood.

The first time in my life that I possessed a feeling of happiness without prejudice or an underlying fear.

I knew at age 16, when I entered 5th year, that I had not had THE easiest or most conventional early years. Albeit I was cared for and loved, it was a decade or more of turmoil and uncertainty for my father and his family. The subsequent emotional and long lasting effects on my mind, my view of adults, the values I had come to appreciate and the principles I had innately engraved in my soul had made it somewhat trying at times to accept things as they were. I knew then that I would spend my entire adult life suppressing my impatience. My lack of understanding as to why people and things can do wrong in the world. My naivety was not global in terms of world peace and poverty, as this is not bespeaking to my worry; but more questionable in terms of my surroundings and why it was we, our family that suffered.

It was at that point I decided that writing, in whatever way I felt natural, would be the opening my soul needed to breathe. Again.

At this age in my life, I was becoming a woman. I had naturally developed. In puberty and in size. I was overeating and still overweight. It was a constant itch I used to avoid scratching. I was in sheer denial and did not want to think about it. I refused to think of all the taunts I had suffered through my earlier school years at Primary AND at Secondary. For most of the perpetrators had now exited school. For a better life, they worshipped.

I was lost. I yearned for the days I could drive, go to University, study, work in a bar, be free, be a student, and be myself. Myself. Be the neurotic, impatient, sensitive, emotional, loyal, enthusiastic and giving soul I had always known I was. However, could not escape my sorrow. It was as if a dagger etched in my heart that I did not have the power to remove. In addition, had to succumb to the presence of time. Allowing time to remove it and relieve me of a burden that I would never ever be enough to people. I was ironically in great belief that one day it would hit me. I would feel inspired by my own freedom and no longer burdened by the abandonment sadness I had unfortunately received as a gift and could never return to sender. No matter how much Elvis Presley sang about it.

Fifth year. The year of Higher Education. And choosing higher courses that would lead me to my chosen profession. Which of course I had no fucking idea was to be. It ranged from Lawyer to Doctor, from Vet to Nurse, from Psychologist to Administrator. I had no idea what or how I would earn my living. What I did know was I badly needed to reign in my eating and lose a few pounds. I was tipping the scales at a manly rate and was wearing a size 16 at 17 years old. Not healthy. I did not know however, what exercise of choice was to transform my body. Therefore, my mum, Morag suggested Aerobics. Tuesday and Wednesday night classes were to transform me. And transform me they did.

I was down at the front of that class jiving to that routine twice a week with the little old woman next to me who attended 5 nights a week. Honestly, she was like wonder woman's granny. And the instructor had abs to die for. Like seriously, I would need to die to actually appreciate that body of hers. But I tried. I tried so hard and I managed to lose a few pounds and gain some confidence. Not too much, but enough to feel like I was making an effort.

Fifth year studies were hard. They really were. I found it difficult managing the optimistic five subjects. So I dropped one; Chemistry. Then the second; History. I stuck with English, Math's and Secretarial Studies. My head was not in it though. I genuinely found it difficult to concentrate. I remember the only redeeming quality about 5th year was my part time work at the weekend. And some new friends I had acquired.

I also discovered McQues that year. McQues, the local public house where the Saturday night dancing was the place to be. Wow. It was carnage but dancing to "think were alone now" by Tiffany was THE highlight of anyone's weekend.

My hair, my short haircut was royally getting on my nerves though. I was at that hairdresser every two weeks having to trim my neck as it was growing fast and looked just ridiculous.

The low point of said haircut came on the fateful day my friend and I decided to go to Edinburgh and audition for Hollyoaks, the popular long running teen set drama series. Open casting call.

OPEN!!!

My friend Heather and I took the train and joined the 4-hour queue. That was a poignant day. I had a tantrum with my hair choosing to NOT sit as I wished it to that day and a remember thinking to myself my choice of top and how it made my boobs look huge might just be the distraction I needed to retain my self-consciousness throughout the audition.

The casting director was looking for a young female to join the show. Young, vibrant, modern, outgoing and witty.

Why the fuck was I there? I had severe poker face. Nevertheless, I mastered my poker face to keep the demons out and the emotions tucked away.

Needless to say after a 4-hour wait, a few quarrels with my friend; ok bitchy arguments might be a better description; a twirl or two by some of the shows existing actors to spruce up the Edinburgh massive who were now losing the will to live in the rain; AND a fateful piece of chewing gum offered by a fellow fame seeker…my turn was next.

The brief; to say your name, your age and where you come from along with something interesting about yourself.
Me: "Melanie, 17, Stirling, Scotland and something interesting is that I have an eidetic memory"

Just at that point,…Chewing gum makes an escape from my mouth, onto the Casting directors' notepad.

"NEXT"

Fail. Big fat fail. Right in the face. Honestly, I should have just stayed at home.

HOWEVER, it was at that precise moment I manage to remove one profession from the list; Actor. Because I was 50 shades of shit.

Little did I know that I would one day be full of humor? Like my dad. *chuckles*

Applications for universities were required by the Spring Semester of 5th year so I had to really think about what courses I wanted to study along with which university I wish to go to. Who would have me? I needed to really think hard about what subject or subjects I wanted to torment my mind with for 4 years. Because it was that dedication that was surely going to earn me the big bucks? Hell to the yes.

I chose Stirling University as my first choice and Edinburgh Napier as my second. Secretly I desired them both and wanted them to want me. And want me they did. With "conditional" offers.

Failed all my highers. Well not all of them. I did ace Secretarial studies but only because I am THE most anal and rigorous person when it comes to details! Did not study hard enough and spent more time on that bloody hairstyle than I did on my subjects though.

But, I was learning to drive. So what more could a teenager want in life!! I also had the Travis Album, a cool part time job AND some decent friends so all was fine. However, I did feel somewhat a failure.

I spent the whole summer giving myself a serious shake. Growing my hair out. And deciding that if I really wanted to go to University, make something of my life and find my own happiness, I needed to eliminate anything and all bullshit that surrounded me.

Therefore, I took on four fresh Highers. Maths, English, Management and Media Studies.

I adored Media Studies. I completely came into my own. Learning to analyze narrative, institutional production, cinematography, advertising and film. Was the happiest period of my week. A double class (2 hours) was my favorite. Mr. Wales was by far THE most influential teacher of my generation. He was on our level; he spoke to us as if we were equals and adults. He inspired us to believe we understood and could command the subject. Moreover, he invested in our education. I thoroughly adored his classes.

The Media studies class taught me how to write clearly. Be articulate and punctual and interpret a short movie excerpt in preparation for the prelim exams.

This was my last chance to achieve great results.

I had a conditional from Stirling University to study Business Law with Psychology. I felt this would give me freedom to research and investigate other mediums/fields of arts/creativity and intellect. At the same time, providing me a Bachelor's degree. I was to be grossly mistaken but more on that later.

I mentally prepared myself of University life. I could not think of anything better than going to university and being an adult.

I was to be joined by my dads' sister, who, at the same age as me, was joining the same university, only from a different school. We were to go together on day 1.

The Common Room. A grand space of retribution and comfort for all seniors in High School.

Or so it was sold.

An utter shit hole in the French corridor where the boys seem to leave everything at their arse and then some. Never tidy. Never clean, never smelling fresh. BUT, Radio 1 blasting every morning and we all felt like adults. A far distance from the pitiful 5th years and anyone below them.

Then the cleaners binned my 6th year Management folder accidentally. ALL OF MY NOTES. Every single bit of study material gone. I was distraught. Because this carried the highest grade in terms of demand from the university. Not to mention I was a complete freak of nature in terms of recording every single detail that would undoubtedly frazzle your mind. Perhaps the cleaner was trying to tell me to calm the fuck down.

Good job I aced that exam and got an A. Eh? Like a boss.

A Management geek was born. The liberating feeling of achieving an A was outstanding. Then I was awarded the Media Studies prize for that full year. As the only school in the region teaching a 6th year Media class, it was a real honor to win something because of my contribution.

It was at that point that I knew my fate lay in the hands of good choices and hard work ethics. Only that. Make a future for myself and continue my road to fulfilment. For the sky would never be the limit when I knew there were footprints on the moon.

6

Freud and fat fashion

At 18 years old, I had acquired an old mind. A traditional and old school values approach to life. I knew deep down I would certainly be one to conform to societal expectation but on the whole, there would be an underlying desire to stay true to my principles. Primarily live an honest, giving, compassionate and generous life. Giving others my time and investment and expect the same in return. Whether that was more ambitious than life would lend me, it was my desire and I never felt like it was asking for more than I rightly deserved in return for my contribution to humanity.

I would still on the odd occasion succumb to the desire to be a total fanny bangle. I am only human after all.

I always had and still have the inability to inflict deliberate hurt or distain on another person. This has meant that at age 18 I was about to embark on a risky 1st year at university with lots of different ages, ethnic minorities, cultures AND I was naturally going to talk to EVERYONE. I could not quite decide whether this was my inner desperation wanting friends or whether I never ever wanted anyone to feel left out. A similar feeling to have been a victim of abandonment.

I should also point out here that when I reference the term "abandonment" I do not use it with aggression or viciousness, more the internal sorrow the feeling left me with.

Luckily, I met two super girls on my first day at University. Both on my business law and Psychology course. They were from different cities/backgrounds and it was enriching chatting about different things to that of high school common room etiquette.

It was with those girls, Helen and Melissa, that I purchased my first Gap Jumper and Freud book on Psychology 101. Both highly pivotal in shaping my style of fashion and educational confusion. Of course, I rocked the red GAP jumper more than necessary but unfortunately was not quite grasping Freud's take on the cognitive movement. Who was he really? Some dude with a cool name. No, only one of the world leading experts on psychological movements. Genius. But by goodness, his name irritated any third or 4th year student I came across. Jung, the alternative was deemed more acceptable in terms of study points of interest. I did not however, discover Jeung until the late noughties when I needed some light Jeung assistance…

I thoroughly engorged myself in Business Law in both Corporate and Delict courses. Or Tort as it is commonly known. I thrived on case studies and the "Smith v Jones 1929" references. The 9am lectures on a Monday morning did not bother me so much as our lecturer had what can only be described as a he-man like body. He did not look like a teacher/professor/lecturer AT ALL. He was a beautiful species to stare at whilst pleading with your memory to understand the complexity of the 10 stages of proving negligence. I shit you not I loved every minute of that course. Scraped by with mediocre but passable grades, because clearly I was a dunce, BUT, it was still a pass so I was on a joyride to legal grandeur I was certain of it!

Ironically this was the era of Ally McBeal. The single most amazing legal show on the TV. Thoroughly enjoyable and I yearned to encapsulate the Ally McBeal style into my own legal showdown. Clearly getting ahead of myself again but god love me for being excited.

I was still shit at Psychology.

I started to think that I was perhaps not as intelligent as most other students. I did however, have a penchant for the business law course. Loved it. And in life, if you love something you are usually good at it if you try hard enough.

Therefore, at age 18, mid-way through my first year I had acquired a few cool things in my early adult life. One, a belly button stud. Every 18-year-old wanted one. I had one. Popped that cherry on my 18th birthday. Even cooler, was an upgraded mobile phone. Nokia bad boy baby. Coolest thing around and had a ringtone and snake the game. Snake II was to be released later that year. How very exciting. FML. Looking back, it stuns me just what managed to entice the young generation. It is frightening how evolution has played a part on societal expectations in genres everywhere.

Secondly, I had acquired a taste for cider. Cider drinking with my university buddies OR my work buddies from the Marches USC. Every weekend I was out. I was actually OUT. Enjoying me, laughing, loving, learning and breaking fashion rules everywhere with my torn jeans and shady denim bandanas.

Mum, why did you allow me to go out like that? Seriously.

The hair was growing though. No more a scary spice reject, just a young student with a questionable in between cuts hairstyle that I decided to experiment with and color all the time.

Unfortunately, though, I had however started a sad journey down a road that led to an eating disorder. I had developed this relationship of hatred with food. All food. Only eating at university and then refusing to eat again for the rest of the day. I drowned myself in water so that I always felt full and smoked one cigarette each day in hopes it would suppress my appetite.

I accepted that I unfortunately possessed this manic need to measure my outlook on everything by a matrix of one end of the scale or the other. Never to dangle in the middle.

The weight started to fall off and I felt skinny. Or skinnier. I had this burning need in me constantly telling me to say no to calories. No matter how weak, unwell, lethargic, dehydrated or hungry I felt. It was an impulsive self-harm that my mind would offset against my genuine happiness at being in a mature environment surrounded by cool students and a student vibe everywhere I went. It was highly unfortunate that my cognition had programmed itself to think that something positive happening in my world surely had to be balanced with something in negative form to remind me that was "where I belonged" and not to get too comfortable. Horrible feeling. Like an unconscious internal prison. Never to be allowed to just have something nice happen or received without "giving back" or "reminding myself" I was just lucky. It ate me. And whilst that feeling ate me, I ate nothing.

I remember that I reverted to morning feeds to fuel my days. Refusing evening meals and walking everywhere. I was still learning to drive and lessons were expensive so walking was good for my campaign to kill my body with starvation kindness. Bittersweet misery was my living hell.

My mornings consisted of an exchange of hellos and goodbyes with my parents as they left for work and I embarked on my one and only feast for the day. A bowl of porridge, two slices of whole meal toast and a cup of tea. Full and ready for the day. A whole 24 hours to pass before I allowed anything else.

I would not allow myself to question my own sanity. Because I knew what I was doing. I was being utterly careless and stupidity had eaten my very last grains of sanity. I had fallen victim to an exaggerated societal presumption that being skinny meant I would be immediately accepted as normal. This shit had been following me for years and now it was manifesting as an eating issue. Surely to end in disaster but as the weight dropped off me I felt alive. I hated myself for enjoying my newfound rib cage. Ironically, I looked like a dead person. My hair was falling out, I looked like a drug addict and my mum plucked up the courage to tell me that I was changing. And not just physically. But personality wise I was becoming short, aggressive, angry, unpleasant and generally not nice to be around. The weight that went took my personality with it. My happy disposition was replaced with an obsessive-compulsive need to count everything, fiercely protecting my feelings and withdrawing from normality.

It was guaranteed to affect my grades and it did.

A chance encounter with a young man at work one weekend meant a shift in my attention and excitement though. This gent was starting his own driving school and through general cashpoint chitchat I had established that he was prepared to offer lessons at cheap prices in hopes of gaining custom. So of course, I jumped at the chance.

He was young, hip, funny and cool. He had an orange Fiat Punto with its own DVD player. COOL AS. I felt like he was more of a friend than an instructor and we had some fun chats together. He taught me discipline when it came to driving and learning. His influence seemed to resonate in my personal life and my struggles with my body that I was desperately trying to hide.

Unfortunately, body changes are rather noticeable especially when your clothes drown you. My skin was now affected and I looked repulsive. However, I was continuously convincing myself I fitted in finally. I was so wrong. And gradually losing my grip on reality.

I wondered how someone so focused on a better life had succumbed to thinking that what I was and what I wanted just was not enough to be accepted. It was crippling for my self-respect and self-consciousness. Highly alarming for anyone around me at that time.

It was not that I felt unloved. I had an abundance of love around me at home. I had people around me at university and at work that were nice enough to me. But I felt empty. It was as if I had a fractured view of my own self-worth and was not sure how to mend that. How to believe that I was worthy of nice things in life? I seemed to acquire this immense guilt for no known reason.

My mum and I decided to venture out for some lunch one day. A "new" for me considering I never ate. We went to a local sports bar that was new, only a couple of years old, but local and had a cool vibe. The service was great. I thought to myself what it might be like to work in that environment. I mean, I was now 18 and could serve a pint. I thought immediately of the social vortex it would open up for me and at that point in what was technically a downward spiral I was convinced this was a great opportunity. I asked for the Manager and freaked the server out. Apologizing profusely, I did advise him it was not related to his service. I asked her for a job. I advised I was a student, local, hardworking and wondered if she would take a chance on me.

How can someone so down and resentful of his or her own being be so confident as to bashfully ask a pub manager for a job? Just like that. I had simply mastered a poker face. Feeling victorious at creating a wall of hidden emotions invisible to other humans. Remaining cool and calm to a strangers' eye and unbeknownst to that person, I had tucked safely in my pocket a world of pain.

She said yes.

She was so much fun to talk with.

The courage that possessed me that day will forever stand in good stead for the people I met in the days/weeks/months to come changed my life forever. I was not a believer in fate in those days, of course, I was not. I was a self-fulfilling control freak. I believe now that particular moment was meant to be. I was meant to ask for a job, I was meant to meet that particular manager and I was meant to begin a new journey pulling pints and learning the meaning of "lager shandy".

It was the beginning of a new era. I just needed to get a grip on my eating and I was certain I had everything under control, in a positive way as opposed to a self-destructive way of life. Because my daily routine at that point was neither healthy nor positive. It bred harm and sorrow. Moreover, it must have been incredibly worrying for my mum and dad. More so, my mum who watched my daily routine closely and never said anything to spark an argument. I will forever be sorry for my selfish existence being a burden on her nerves. As I am sure, she worried constantly about my emotional state of mind.

It never crossed my mind once that I might be suffering from a severe childhood depression. A depression never treated, that had gotten worse the longer it lay dormant in my fragility. I will never know if I did, still do or might do in the future. What I do know is that coming months enabled me to interact in a calmer and assuring way with my parents, my friends, my university teachers and me. I can only liken it to having crippling nerves around everything and everyone and constantly suspecting everyone and everything for the fear, "they are out to get you". In addition, managing to slowly release each one of those demons, day by day. One by one. I wanted to believe that those people with the worst pasts created the best futures. Fully appreciating that my past was not horrific. It was just painful. To me, to my heart, to my ability to mend emotionally and rebuild the ability to enter into relationships in all lifestyles with no worry or anxiety. A feat that will never cease to be at the forefront of my adult mind.

My first day on the pint pulling job seen love and me meet a girl ill know until the day I die.

What a gem. Crabbit bitch on first glance right enough but a friendship was soon born. Her name? Samantha Hume. It amazes me how poignant a first impression is and can be when it becomes apparent pretty quickly that a friendship is brewing. She cleaned section 2 of that bar so well, I wondered if she was an army sergeant in secret. She oozed wit and charm and I enjoyed her personality. Circumstance was to part us for a brief time but a solid sisterhood was formed because of course she was a *Hume.*

It always amazes me, that on that very first day, that I can recall the exact date, time, place, smells, characteristics of certain introductions. There was also a manager who had obviously just finished her shift. She had this outrageous bleached blonde hair. I thought to myself, she is a bold chick. She was reading page 10 of the Sun and eating vanilla ice cream. She had that "do not fucking dare approach me to clean anymore sick from the toilets or serve any more burgers to table 10, I have done my shift now do one" look on her face. I immediately liked her. I introduced myself to her.

We have also been friends for many years now, minus the 2.75 years we did not speak because both of us were too stubborn to admit any fault. It was mostly mine for being a fool in love and choosing bros before hoes. My mistake.

My university life was dwindling though. Like your legs after three jaeger bombs. I was losing interest in University the more I worked a night shift in the pub. The banter I had was irreplaceable in a 9am lecture on contract law.
Getting to know regulars and how they liked their lager tops was a joy. Yes, the pay was a pittance but I was a student living at home and any income was still an income. It fed my active social life and contributed to my first car.

Finally, I passed my test. Third time around.

I blame my first failure on the fact that I had my very first adult date that same night. (I say adult, because I refused to date until I was old enough and emotionally stable enough to keep a lid on my shit in public!) A member of staff in the pub I worked for. Sent me flowers and everything that morning. What a sweetheart. I was mind blown. Forgetting of course I was about to sit my driving test. What a fool. There was me not paying attention to anything on the road. For I was being taken on an actual date that very evening. A girl is allowed to be excited though right?

Do you remember your first date as an adult?

I had not been without male attention, do not get me wrong. However, as an adult with a real anxiety and emotional turbulence occupying substantial space in my mind; it was utterly enticing to have some hot boy pay me attention. Even if he only wanted to get me naked. Of which I like to believe was not his intention. He had however dated two people I knew through the grapevine. They both advised against it but I was an old romantic, beneath and behind all my irrational bravado. That had and will never leave my soul. To be romantic. To know that the ship will always turn around, even in the darkness.

He sent flowers to me. What the actual fuck. Knock at the door and the flowers arrived. Royally shitting all over my "must pass my driving test" A game. Royally. I got around 35 minors. I was a danger to society and my instructor looked at me with sheer distain! Like I had urinated on his cornflakes.

I like to look back on that day with fondness. That my instructor, G, felt pity that something so nice was happening for me that day. It just was not the joyous "pass" we had worked so hard for. It was another "pass". A pass go straight into the dating scene.

I dread to think what people must have actually thought about me. They must have thought I was an utterly crazy chick. But loveable nonetheless. Surely right? I reckon so.

I may have been emotionally challenged BUT I seemed to have an ability that attracted people to my person and they stayed. In terms of longevity and friendship. Could not keep a man for love nor money, not that I had any (HA), but I seemed to possess a shine that did not diminish and I had good souls around me. Both in terms of my family and close network, and with new friends I had made in the pub industry. It was a small community and very clique like but I was overcome with excitement and desire at figuring out whom floated my irrationally challenged boat and kept me afloat.

I developed a great relationship with the chefs. For they knew to make me steamed carrots and tortilla wraps when I was hungry. Just enough carbs and calories to suppress my starvation but not too many that the guilt erupted in my conscience like a volcano on speed. How they managed to get through a shift without condemning me for being such an utter moron is beyond me. They must have surely thought to themselves, she is not normal. Although they might not have given two hoots. I will never know.

Could you imagine if I had been medicated and you would never have the pleasure of reading such a joyously humorous tale of an unknown author writing her life story? Cool right? Oh, it gets better. More shit to follow!

Laugh. Out. Loud. Do it with me.

Flip-flops became my obsession. I had so many pairs and my feet felt free. It was like my feet were the gateway to my soul and only free speech allowed escaping from my person. Therefore, multi colored footwear, even in winter, was my thing. Fashionista baby. I had the most terrible toenails though. I painted them that much, repeatedly that, the nail bed was screaming blue murder for a day off. They stopped growing and instead of seeking the proper attention, I just cut them off and kept painting. I am a stupid *stupid* girl. Well, I was. But I rocked multi colored toenails in December. Never a sock was seen. However, an abundance of distain and disapproving looks from my mum came frequently. Fascinated by my newfound flat stomach I found it necessary to flaunt said stomach at any opportunity. It was slowly becoming painfully obviously my desire to be a scholar was quickly being replaced with being a minor stripper. In a manner of speaking. So even in my darkest hour from a 'desperate to be accepted and considered normal' point of view, I actually enjoyed feeling like I had a shape. Albeit a malnourished shape.

I had also developed a liking for dark eye make-up. Circa Friends 1998. That and a pair of ultrasonic curling tongs meant for 3-hour glamour routine for even a walk to the shops.

Ironically, I had become somewhat fanatical about being groomed to perfection all the time.

Collection 2000 make up was the brand I wore because, well basically, it was all I could afford. Collection 2000, the only way to resemble something from the 80's. But I hid my features like a true professional. In those days, of course there was no contouring, no duck face, no pouting lips and no ritualistic obsession with the thick eyebrow. However, I liked to plaster that shit on my face like a mask and felt utterly butterly. It was a crying shame my frizzy excuse for a hairstyle never did play ball. Never really had a style.

But I had a set of crimpers.

I swear to Lucipher they produced some outstanding hairstyles. Crimped hair for a night out. I should have been medicated. Or sectioned. Or both! Who in their right mind crimps their hair? I was 19 years old and clearly auditioning for my own girl band. Except I could neither sing nor move like Beyoncé.

Then came the day I decided to try peroxide. Bleach blonde. What a big fat kick in the stones that was. Not that I have stones but if I had it would surely have resembled the pain I felt when I looked in the hair salon mirror and scoffed at just what monstrosity I had become. It was bloody awful. My dark roots were showing already and the color had only been on about 7 minutes. It is as if you are on a stopwatch with peroxide and you only get your fair ration. "Quick, dry, go, swan about town and then boom, back in the salon seat for another 60 quid update to your horrendous mop".

I was yet to discover GHD's. The 21st century's answer to the definition of nice hair.

Therefore, my hair was generally up. Hair up, dark eyes, looking gaunt. A walking twenty first century Addams Family value. Wednesday Addams personified.

How did I have friends? Or people engage in conversation when I looked that frightening.

Then there was the fake tan. Or racially challenged bronzer. That I of course chose to sport every living moment of my 19th year. You could see me in the dark. With my bright white smile and my pale white feet always on show, I should have been a pop star. I had all the delusions in place. But god love me for exuding some warped sense of confidence for once in my adult life.

Remember these were the days that there was no Photoshop, no filters, no Instagram. I have the photographic proof hidden in a dark cell in the pits of my secret world, guarded by 24-hour lockdown security in fear of those fantastic bad boys coming to life and shaming me into an early grave. Oh how I thank the lord daily for Instagram. And any other photos filter APP. More on SELFIES later.

The part time nightlife existence I had become enthralled in was changing me. For the better in terms of my social circle and the joys that made me smile every time I entered that solitude. For the worse in terms of my self-analysis of my body and how that pain never left my mind. And was never shared with anyone.

Except my colleague. Who on February 10 2001 took me to one side whilst I was wearing a size 10 Topshop fitted shirt that was baggy. She looked me straight in the eye and said; "Mel, I can see your ribs". She could as well. I could. My mum could. My inner hatred refused to acknowledge I was starving myself to death.

My hair was falling out. Falling out fast. I disguised it by inventing cool new styles every day. My job required me to tie my hair back for hygiene reasons so it was hidden well. Obviously, my body told an astonishingly different tale of a forgotten fatty. Turned anorexic wannabe.

I should have at that point invented a brand called Fatfascination. It was all I thought about.

I needed a wakeup call. That came the day I sadly realized I was failing my University course, my attitude to life was dwindling because I had crippling exhaustion and malnourishment gripped by body like a drowning wave. It was a moment-to-moment struggle to stay awake longer than a few hours each day without feeling immense fatigue.

My mum looked at me with such sadness in her eyes. What had her girl become. What had years of feeling such self-loathing done to this kind hearted, sensitive soul. Who only ever wanted to feel good enough? To feel loved. To feel accepted. To feel worthy.

Not a single soul knew what I was hiding internally. However, I needed help. I was a walking example of how to allow negativity and past pain destroy the road to happiness. Although that in itself irritated me. That I saw happiness as a point of destination as opposed to a living daily self-realization. It had to change. And for the better. If I was to ever become something, feel something, desire something and accomplish any dreams that lay dormant and suffocated, I had to accept my choices were the only decisions that mattered. Mistakes would be made, and had been in abundance, but I needed to venture out from under my rock of misery and get a fucking grip on my personality. Which had been nicked by the artful dodger some years ago.

7

The art of rejection

Change was not to happen overnight. Unfortunately writing this in my thirties, it still is not completely resolved. Because we live in a society of expectations and demands on our being. On our physical appearance and how we dominate our immediate surroundings by the choices we make in using that physical appearance for the good. Or for the bad. Or in many cases for the indifferent.

I was prepared for an awakening. However, fueled by alcohol and a habitual routine of socializing with my work colleagues on a Friday and Saturday, either pre-empted or followed by a shift in the pub, I had a burning desire to feel attended to. I craved a love so deep the world's oceans would be jealous. Being a teenager though meant I was to embrace a more casual style of discovery in terms of the opposite sex. Little did I know that attracting boys came with a specific etiquette you had to acquire through careful study.

This did not come naturally to me. A bit like my eyelashes. Why GOD why.

From the secret cloakroom hook-ups to the innocent glances across the nightclub dance floor, the piercing reality of true love that everyone was and still is looking for that something to catch their eye. My eyes were popping. From dancers to DJ's to door stewards to colleagues to fellow students and to random people, I found myself drawn to a particular type. Tall, sturdy and large looking people with a rough and ready look about them. I did not fall victim to the "tall, dark and handsome" facade. I was not that deluded. In reality, I was probably swinging down the other end of the spectrum with my serious lack of appreciation of 21st century dating. I harbored such a negative opinion about dating and how deceit is the number one checkpoint in the decision making process. I stand by the notion though that people are STILL unable to be as brutally honest as they are to themselves. For example, why is it so hard to say, "I am just not that into you" or "I am sorry I do not find you attractive"? Instead "I am seeing someone" (when you are not) or "I am not looking for anything at the moment" (when you clearly are).

Why is it that the need, desire and want to capture that butterfly feeling of being someone's someone, even only briefly, somehow resonates with your inner soul and conscience when delivering bad news to someone who's feelings you do not reciprocate? In my humble opinion, this is human decency. On the other hand, for want of a more social friendly word; a filter.

Filters. Allowing you to distort reality. Because deep down my reality at this time was hidden. On the inside anyway. If not on my physicality. Broken, rib showing, hair loss, gaunt drug addict sorry looking lost soul I was. Still managing attracting attention in the male form.

Filters. Allowing you to seem like you are something you are not. Because married men or women are not somehow stopped from approaching those other than their spouse. Choices. Everyone is responsible for his or her own.

Filters. Allowing suppression of true feelings, whether good, bad or ugly, from translating into verbal language having travelled from your conscious mind to your mouth.

The latter the most important at that point.

It always amazed me, and still does how society/upbringing/surroundings teach you basic interaction etiquette however; you always were and are capable of blasphemy when perhaps dealing with a crazy driver in front of you or your stub your toe. As well as anger, when you feel passionately about something. But, there is an innate filter when someone directly asks you on a date/for a kiss/to buy you a drink; and when you immediately decide that you aren't interested; most people's reaction is to filter or distort the answer so as to not inflict unnecessary hurt or pain on that person. I admire and wholeheartedly appreciate that being something that resonates with most. The choice not to further embarrass someone who has perhaps gone through their own journey in assuming the courage to tell you how they feel about you. Yes, you.

Why is that? Do you think we are all born with compassion to protect others from feeling rejected?

I like to think it is a far bigger sentiment.

I have often analyzed that these types of situations call for empathy and tact. Because deep down, in the pits of your sub-conscience we all want the same thing. To share our soul with its counterpart in another. Whether you admit that or not.

This is not about marriage or milestones. This pertains to the feeling of love. In love, desiring love, wishing for love, feeling loved, giving love and basking in a sea of utter harmony.

So, when faced with a situation where you are only able to offer rejection as an answer to the question, it sure does give me comfort that generally society are equipped with the ability to tailor the standard "not interested" to the particular person based on body language and various other factors.

Then there are the occasions where the requestor is a total lune ball, has accosted you in an either drastically over the top manner or has inappropriately detailed every single sexual act he would like to do to you. You are of course forced to reach into your pocket and bring out "bitch mode".

"Go fuck yourself" is an all-time outstanding comeback. Then you feel mortified that you will undoubtedly attract attention from other people. (The scene here is a bar for example).

"Why are you following me" is slightly more alarming if you are walking a dark street. However, let us pretend that never happens. Please.

So, you are faced with a choice. Tell this douche to go and actually fuck themselves or politely but firmly decline their offer in hopes that they do indeed vacate your personal space and never darken your door again. Sadly, with a particular type of arrogant twat, both are guaranteed to draw a reaction of anger, insult and offence…

I used to take said reactions really badly and to heart.

I remember this one time a man brushed past me in a club when I was 19. Now my immediate reaction was not to scream bloody murder simply because a member of the opposite sex touched my body. My immediate reaction was to see if that said person a) was attractive in my eyes and b) was doing it deliberately and not just politely trying to maneuver around a very busy venue. Sad as it may seem, had he been handsome I would of course not have minded. Nevertheless, he was not to my satisfaction even though I had established he was keen by his rather suggestive use of his tongue and body language from afar.

Now, the suffragist in me dictates that regardless of his royal hotness, I should have adopted the same attitude to a man touching my body without permission. However, the hussy and horny teenager in me adopted a simpler form of decision-making. If he is hot, he is in. If he is not, he is out. Simples.

Perhaps not in this situation.

He is suggestive. He is shaking his tongue at me in what I can only describe as the same motion used when eating an iced lollipop. Gross right? Yeah, this is in an open bar on a Friday night. It is not his look but the predatory aura that is off-putting. The choice I inevitably made was to ignore him. Bad move, he approached me, asked if I would like a drink and after a slight pause (shock factor), I replied "no thanks I am with my friends". My inner patience and manners meant I chose a polite yet appreciative choice of words by way of rejection. Because he is just a person looking for a girl, same as me right. Of course, I am a little embarrassed and touched that someone has shown me interest. I think that it is human nature and anyone so arrogant to lack possession of some human decency is a fool at that.

Wrong. He was a guy looking to get a cheap lay and had made his move on me. Although instinctively deep down I found an internal struggle to offer immediate insult to scare him off. I found it hard to automatically tell him to go away. I felt a natural desire to remain polite. I think nowadays when I reminisce I conclude this surely must have been because I did not want to draw attention to the situation right? Actually, I am certain it is more to do with my genetic programming. Fine-tuned over many years and essentially created and instilled as part of my growing into adulthood.

So why would he not leave me alone?

Because he was unprepared for rejection? Because he felt, he deserved a yes. Because he has never been told no thanks before? Alternatively, was it really, because he felt I expressed sheer audacity at turning him down?

His response to to my polite rejection: "what! You aren't even that nice anyway and you are a fat mess".

Wow. So now, there are several people aware that this dude is having a go at me. And for what? For saying no thanks. What if I had said yes? Would that tongue, belonging to that moron, be licking my face? I shudder to think.

The immediate moments following that were a blur. Have you ever self-analyzed every fraction of your being in a space of around 5 seconds over words that someone else has afforded you by way of attack? Have you ever stood and thought shit is that all true? Shit, does everyone else think that too? Am I a fat mess? Because I did.

What had started at around 8pm as a pleasant entrance to a venue, approach to the bar, removing of my jacket and casually glancing around the room; had become an uncomfortable pit of destruction aimed at me for daring to say no. And for why? Because I dented his fucking ego. What a dick.

Therefore, you see you can be the most naturally pleasant, patient and understanding of hopeless romantics, but faced with attack on your disposition and physicality, unbeknownst to him something I had a minute-by-minute struggle with; I lost my shit. I lost it. I brought all fury and verbal outrage from the depths of my stomach up through my mouth and straight into the face or this sorry excuse for a man.

Was it alcohol enticed? Perhaps. Was he obnoxious but maybe a little handsome? Perhaps. Was his looks and alcohol levels justification for being so very cruel unreasonably, to a woman he has never met? Absolutely not.

Does that sentiment happen to both genders? Absolutely. And are both species to blame for setting standards so low (and high for many other reasons) that dating has become one of lives many puzzles. And headaches.

And I would be lying if I said that society has gotten any better. Or me for that matter. Still faced with these challenges, even more so with social media invading our doorsteps since 2007, it has become a world of filters. Filters that mold your every move.

Because even though we are all just walking each other home, we are still wondering whose hand to hold for the journey...

Put your tissue away and stop chuckling. It was not and is not all bad. I was deeply wounded by the fat mess reference but generally, that situation taught me more than it offended me. Thankfully.

As a 19-year-old, I felt I had an old soul. I was all too aware of my shortcomings in terms of how I was taking care of my body. Ironically, for years I was overweight and not taking care of my body. Now, I was underweight, starving and miserable and thus, not taking care of my body. Nevertheless, I had an innate understanding about happiness and what was required to feel that. Yet, I possessed such denial.

Acceptance. A feeling I never felt truly lived in my heart. But one I afforded to all those around me. I often gave too much of it away. Too quick to accept, too quickly to believe, too quickly to say yes and too quickly to switch up my mood at the merciful hands of another. Essentially allowing someone else to control the puppetry of my contentment and feeling of satisfaction.

I was a 19-year-old boy-come man's dream. Charm her and she will say yes. And charmed I felt, so yes I came a running. Why is that so sad? Literally and realistically. After all society teaches about being a "strong woman" why was I so quick to conform to what *they* desired. Was I desperate and craving a loss of affection? Was I needy and prepared to say, do or be anything a man wanted. Even sexually? Even casually? I probably was. If I could bottle the feeling I had when I received a morning or goodnight text, a glaring look of affection, a man choosing to spend his time with me, me! I certainly would. And I would sell it a dime a dozen as I am certain it would sell. Then we wouldn't really need a companion would we? Yes, denial is reserved for Egypt and the gullible. Get it? Not the

Country, the river. Dafty.

A hopeless romantic and wannabe someone's someone. Yet at 19, my focus was my body, studying, partying and sleeping. I occasionally smoked my friends' cigarettes. Okay, I smoked them excessively and at about a fiver a pack in those days she looked at me as if I had drowned her puppy and that I was lucky she loved me. Because I never bought any. Not ever.

Nights out, tequila shots, archers' aqua bottles, apple sours, DJ Sammy and his rocking remixes and the horrific hangovers were undoubtedly the best platform for meeting some of my epic conquests.

From the DJ's to the dancers to the door attendants, one-night hook-ups seemed to be the popular trend. And that was the early 00's. I knew my mum was all too aware I was promiscuously engaging in rascal shenanigans on a weekend night, but remained polite and calm in her approach to "how was your night". She knew. She bloody knew. She did it herself back in the day. Back in the actual day my friend, she did no doubt love life as if I was now.

She did not have a mobile phone the size of your hand back in those days though. The only avenue and means of communicating at 10p per message on a pre-paid basis. 10p per message. So ten quid was not getting you far if you rabbited on as much as I did. With my university friends, with anyone that replied!

A mobile phone was the only gateway to your social status in 2001. That was a pinnacle year for me. Having a list of speed dial contacts, a malnourished body, male attention and a love for carrots and tortilla wraps. It is any wonder I was not happy!

Nevertheless, I did have the ability to run that bar on a Saturday day shift as Maria ran those Von Trapp kids. Raindrops on roses and Stella on bar top! Boom. I was a girl on a mission. And I was soon promoted to supervisor. What a crock of shit that was. The banter on a day shift was epic though. The football was always on; the regulars were in by 11.30am and the loud lads arrived for lunch in their favorite booth overlooking the large screens around noon. That was where my flawless hair and makeup said goodbye love, goodbye happiness. I swear I aerobically worked my arse every single Saturday day shift and it is any wonder I consumed so much alcohol after each shift. To sedate my crazy mind for coping with glasses piling up, punters shouting for a fresh pint, kegs running out of Bud and not a single soul in sight to help me. I am certain on occasions I felt like I was having a meltdown.

I had rhythm though. I knew my way around the whole venue. The restaurant, the bar, the cellar, the entertainment center, the office, the DJ booth (ahem!), the toilets. The whole place was a 2nd home and the people in it reminded me what it was like to feel alive.

I struggled every day though. In silence. With chronic loneliness and desperation to be liked. To feel adored.

Was my absent mother from years gone by in youth having such an impact on my ability to trust that abandonment is infrequent? Or was and (still) is my mind occupied and at time consumed by the fear and anxiety of always feeling alone?

I never felt lonely in my car. God bless my Nissan Micra. White K reg Nissan Micra. Some girls' first car is like girls' first dress, first bra, and first mobile phone. It is all shiny and new and everyone pays you compliments.

My radio cassette player on high alert and breaking glass whilst bouncing at full volume on my 5-minute drive to work day in day out. Because remember I am a university drop out at this point. Cruising the streets looking like something out of "The Scheme". Good grief. And let me tell you fuel was not cheap either. Back in the day of 2001-NOW, it was and is no cheap matter filling up your car with unleaded and weeping as your bankcard kisses you goodbye as it takes a suicide dive off the forecourt roof. For your sheer abuse and lack of affection. Bad times.

In my case, everyone wants you to play taxi. I never minded though. I loved driving. I used to always forget to put my lights on at night though. EVEN though I had to drive by the Police Station. It was as if my subconscious femme fatale wanted to be caught, be banged up and be handcuffed by PC McHot Stuff. Chance would have been a fine thing. Ironically, the Police Station was located directly next door to the Driving Test Centre and although I was a mere new driver; I STILL found me incapable of basic night driving rules. What a muppet.

Perhaps it was my exhaustion having worked so many long hours, eating only carrots, tortilla wraps and porridge AND the fact that smoking had not yet been banned inside venues so arriving home each night smelling like a chimney was hardly enticing for my fresh nostrils and bed sheets.

The routine of working mostly night shifts following my exit from university quickly became monotonous and mundane. Compounded by my lack of income, and in 2001 a very low national minimum wage; I did wonder what I would make of my life. I had worked so hard at school to get decent grades. Why was I not I able to commit fully to a degree? Why didn't I possess the strength to just get on with it? Why were the nightlife scene and the chance of new friends who liked me for me more appealing than any long-term future planning?

It dawned on me daily I just wanted to be loved. To be happy. To feel content. To feel like getting out of bed in the morning and not allowing my inner sorrow to drown me on that particular day.

I wrote a diary. However, I became quite resentful that all I seem to put in it were negative thoughts. Thoughts about my body, about my hatred for people who were cruel to me. For my grudge against those in school who were mean and bullied me into self-loathing. I carried that weight on my shoulders even at 19 years old. Weight. Weight was all around me. No matter how loose my clothes were.

I had an impulsive nature in that I would find myself having clean, tidy, make everything neat and perpendicular or I could not relax. Not quite clinical OCD but heading down that road for sure.

Decided to paint my room. Bearing in mind my sister has long moved out and I am in the small room. So lilac wallpaper, yellow skirtings' and a brand new bed was to make for a chirpy 19-year-old college drop out with an emaciated body and lack of ambition for future earnings.

8

Social vortex

Turning 20 was somewhat victorious. I had managed to make it out of teenage ninja years unscathed.

I only had a real issue with people, romance, body image, ambition and the resounding voice in my head asking where I go now! So not all bad. She says with sarcasm rife.

"University drop out 20-year-old female seeks a wakeup call" Should have been written on my forehead. I know that now. It is amazing how fractured your open mindedness can become when you allow your mind to consume itself with all that is wrong with you and with the world. I could not at that point think of anything that would have been more welcome than someone telling me to really take a step back and view my life. A lack of maturity mixed with naivety certainly occupied full space in my mind for the most part of my 19th year.

And then our little cat died. Yes, we had a cat. A stray cat called Pussy. She just appeared one day and we took her in. She was so loveable and fun to play with. And the times she sat on my lap, I cherished. I am and always was meant to be a cat lover. I guess most people are either cats or dogs. Some like shady things like tarantulas but hey, each to their own. I shan't be marrying a tarantula or python owner! What fun do these pets actually bring? I really should ask an owner. And arrange to discuss that with them AWAY from their place of home. I cannot be sitting talking trash about my arachnophobia and Mr. chuckles the eight –legged tarantula is waiting to unleash all venom on my sorry ass.

So cats it was. Cats it still is and cats it always will be.

Pussy was run over one night outside our house. I was working a day shift but when I got home, I knew something was wrong. No one was around and that was unusual, even for the cats' standard! She was always eating. Wee fatty. Then my mum appeared. Red and puffy eyed. Poor Pussy had been run over and was dead. Little might. I was devastated. And so was my mum.

It is amazing how drawn and attached one can become to an animal. Especially animals like cats and dogs who arguably communicate with you through their eyes, the tilting of their head, their purring and their barking. We were so attached to her and would miss her terribly. I swore to myself that I would most definitely adopt a cat of my own one day.

My colleagues and friends at work were compassionately supportive. Which was really very much appreciated considering it was an animal and they did not know her. But I think it does not actually cost a person anything but their time to just show empathy at times like that.

I found comfort in USC Miss Sixty bell-bottom jeans. What the actual fuck? Size 10 though no less. Never one to allow the focus of my malnourished existence to shit all over my new jeans parade. I resembled something out of the 70's based film Boogie Nights, except with clothes. Not naked. And not auditioning for a Dirk Diggler extra...

Sixty quid down the drain. Earning 500 pounds, a month was a misery. I had reached that point where it was only fair that my parents benefit monetarily from my full time income, as I was no longer a poor student. Still poor. Just not protected by the circle of education any longer. God dammit! It was a hardship having to part with nearly half my income just for the sheer joy of continuing to live at home. Looking back now, I fully recognize the selfish disposition that undoubtedly possessed me in my utter fury at parting with those bucks monthly. However, boy did my mum Morag cook a mean meal. Beautiful.

Takes me back to that Christmas. Freezing so it was. And remember I am the countries newest spokesperson for year round flip-flop wearing. Or so I would have everyone think. And Christmas Day was no exception.

Christmas Eve, done a back shift in the pub. Sporting the festive uniform, a rather snazzy glittery top and my trousers that hung of my hips like a 2-year-old having a tantrum. Hair stinking, sweat running down my face, collection 2000 makeup gone to the promise land a mere 20 minutes into my shift because the pub is that busy we are all inhaling each others breath. Ding. The bells come. And true to form the Christmas songs that play all over the world, in every home, venue, radio station etc. it was no exception. The Pogues ft. Kirsty MacColl beams out Fairytale of New York and I start to get emotional. It never fails the impact the words of that song have on me. Still to this day, it reminds me of harmony. Of a happy feeling. Sitting around the Christmas tree thinking about the carrots and biscuit along with ice-cold milk you desperately wanted Santa to enjoy. Even though at a young age you have no idea about bad that was for his cholesterol. Hilarious.

So, I am serving happy punters as the clock strikes midnight and it is a happy environment. Customers and staff alike are joyous in their celebration of the arrival of the big man in the red suit. He did not actually appear you understand. He was obviously too busy out sleighing all over Plean.

"And the bells were ringing out for Christmas Day" (Ref; Pogues ft. Kirsty MacColl) and the tune that accompanied those lyrics made and still make me feel a real sense of unity. Whether around colleagues, friends or family.

Made a few tips that night. Enough to fuel my car. My little white Nissan Micra. The most expensive asset in my life. And boy was petrol not a royal burden on anyone's finances. Made a verbal tip as well… "Go easy on the eyeliner Mel". Aye ok Steve. Steve, a local in the bar. Never out the bar. Avid Chelsea fan. Always in for soccer Saturday. Clearly had a penchant for people's eye make-up. Perhaps he was a qualified make-up artist in disguise.

So I quickly rush to the washroom thinking oh shit, have the sweat, blood, excitement and blazzeh approach I have to Christmas Eve had an effect on my makeup and am I secretly reminiscent of the 80's singers who painted their faces black and white. I shuddered to think so off I scurried to the washroom only to be met by a squander of girls in the toilets doing to the obligatory "oh my god I love your shoes", "oh my god you should see that guy".

You girls know what I mean. 'Those girls you meet in toilets'. A whole universe of unity and feminism right there.

You know those awkward introductions that you so easily emulate when faced with a queue in a bathroom for the actual toilet, sink OR indeed the dryer. People who, normally may never enter your life as a friend or foe, but in that vortex of bowel heaven, you are somewhat socially compelled to make eye contact. Small talk. But, in the truest and quickest form of flattery, you always immediately strike up a conversation about someone's shoes, dress or hair. Don't you? Do not deny it girls.

And there you have it. You have exchanged names. Sarah, 22 student, size 4 feet, works in the local chippie, studying economics, lives on campus, dating a rugby boy, has her period, feeling low, but has new shoes on. Boom, you have acquired a synopsis of her key selling points in a matter of 23 seconds, and you are smitten. Like a dog to a chew toy. You have moved to a "perched" body disposition and are gorged in a one-on-one chat with this girl as if she is your long lost relative. And all the time you are absolutely bursting for a pee that has now started to trickle down your leg. However, you care not a sausage. For Sarah is a joy. Her stories of woe were exciting and refreshing. I found myself sharing my life with her. About my failed university course, my starvation diet of carrots and tortilla wraps, the fact that I was living in a bedroom at home painted yellow and lilac and have recently discovered that having lilac all around you is a sign of depression; AND to top it all off have just been told that I resemble the lead singer from Kiss. But she cares not a sausage either! A true friendship is born. And what is it about those bathroom introductions that leave such a bittersweet feeling of offering an olive branch of quick unprecedented friendship? I believe it is the idea that any scenario can and will lead you to the events that scope your being. And Sarah, who I was completely enamored by, opened up my mind to see that I was not alone in my questionable daily dramas. She too had the naivety complex I so easily ruled as part of my overall neurosis. I loved her. She made me giggle. I decided yes. Yes, I definitely need her chat in my life. Going forward Sarah and I will be firm friends. And so we made plans to call each other the following day.

Never heard from her again.

I completely omitted to realize that girl was out on Christmas Eve, shitfaced 3 sheets from the wind and completely unaware of her own name. Which I only see from her driver's license she dropped when her bag made an attempt at hungry hippos all over the bathroom floor.

Not to mention it was Christmas Day.

I did not feel rejection far from it. Reality check on life. That the funniest of encounters can and did teach me about foundations of relationships and how they can stem from nothing and from everything.

And then it was Christmas Day. Me and my flip-flops sought solace and joy in the Christmas Now Album and that of the joyous feast that my mum prepared. That day and every Christmas Day. With little burnt chipolata sausages, that Ashleigh held ransom then and even now. She traded them off like some London meat market trader. "Right Mel I will trade you my 2 potatoes and some carrots for your two chipolatas". Why mum did not just give her a plate full of sausage for dinner is beyond me. That alone would have made her Christmas. For in spite of all her faults she is so easily pleased. So laid back. Little sausage diva.

I however loved them so. And refused. But I am certain she stole mine on occasion.

Christmas presents at that age were outstanding though. Always were but especially as we were getting older. Things like mobile phones, computers, expensive shoes or boots, vouchers for River Island, stereos, shit you just did not need but that was cool to have. Loved Christmas. My parents definitely did not. Our demands were often extreme and I apologized to them now for expecting so much. Sorry Dad. And Mum. I am not sorry for the sausage demands though. That was necessary.

And trifle. Homemade strawberry trifle so effortlessly made with such finesse on Christmas Eve was and to this day still is the masterpiece of Hume Christmas. A layer of whipped cream, a layer of custard and a layer of Cadburys Flake. The Flake though we had to and again still have to remind mum to buy leading up to Christmas. She is getting old you see. Forgets and then all hell breaks loose over the trifle that is fed bare of its "angel on top of the tree". Just does not taste the same. In addition, we were always quick to judge and critique, which I am sure, pleased her no end. Like the time I stole her vodka.   But not this Christmas. A picture of sheer beauty. Each mouthful enriching the taste buds in true harmony. Closing your eyes to enjoy the fruitful taste of berries, cream, custard and Cadbury's. Forgetting that we have all just devoured two courses of essential perfection in our starters of prawn cocktail and salad AND the the traditional Christmas Turkey with every trimming known to mankind. Not to mention the shared gravy dispenser that makes its way around the table like a cheap whore being passed about before she is empty and void of all emotion.

Tasty feasting. Topped off by Trifle. A glorious day.

My friend joined us for Christmas Dinner that day. She did have family but quite a distance away and she was to work the Christmas Day evening shift. Therefore, I trotted off to drop her at work (flip-flops in full swing!) only to return to my harmonious cocoon of purple wallpaper, yellow skirtings' and a new VHS boxset of Friends season six. Remember that season. God remember that show? Can hardly believe it ended in 2004. As

I write this that is 11 years ago.

I often think back to 2004 and how the fashion in Friends final season was on point. Far more advanced than it was in contemporary society and how if you watched it back now you would think it was made in the late noughties. God bless the effects that show had and probably still has on many a generation.

Season 6, the year Elle MacPherson played a pivotal part. Amazing. The color in that season I have always found the most enticing to watch. How strange is it that I looked at the overall artistry of the sets with such analysis that I am certain that it is that season and all its imagery that fueled my long running desire to live in Manhattan.

It is highly ironic that not a single episode was filmed in the state of New York. Although the perception still to this day engulfs my ambition with pipe dream fueled hopes and faith it will be my reality one day. One day.

I watched around 12 episodes that night. Which at 22 minutes an episode (removing the breaks and owning that fast forward button like a boss); it only took around 5 hours. Nevertheless, in conjunction with a full box of mint matchmakers, a box of pringles and heavenly amounts of juice, the final hours of my Christmas night were glorious.

Until my sister and I decided to venture out. Precisely how my food baby and bulging tummy (not to mention the sheer irony that at my most neurotic starvation stage of life I ate a full three course dinner), did not squander all interest of partaking in a Christmas extravaganza up town is beyond me. So off we both get ready and head out. It is arguably - 35 degrees and our nipples were like bullets in the snow. Oh my actual God. Flip flops you are no doubt asking? Yes, sir. Flip flops and bell-bottom jeans. And a penchant for the vodka so my sister and I (on one of only a few life long nights out, we have shared just the two of us!) are up that town giving it laldi. Scottish readers will know exactly what I mean by that.

Quietest night ever. Clearly all the other over eating, Quality Street munching; only fools and horses and huge Christmas day special fans chose the warm and cozy option of staying home, as we should have. Or I should have anyway. I am certain Ashleigh was not having that great a time but she only lived along the road in town so she could get home easy. I had to stand in the queue for a cab. On Christmas night. Now you are thinking since it was quiet my experience will have no doubt been easy. Wrong. Why is it that the experience etiquette you apply to the "meeting people in toilets" never applies to those you meet in the taxi queue?

The taxi queue. Where the fun comes to die. There is always someone with something horrible to say. And on the day of Santa no end. Ruined my buzz.

Fortunately, I had some matchmakers, Quality Street and the rest of a Friends box set awaiting me at home.

In addition, having just bought a new bed, mattress, bedding and JAMMIES, I was all set for a shower, a snuggle and an imaginary cuddle from Pussy. Poor Pussy.

Therefore, the weeks that followed Christmas seen me earn some real tips in the land of bright lights and Stella tops. The prison that became my home. My earner, my land of acquaintances, income, tortilla wraps and head office big wigs.
Big wigs that did transfer me to another unit to work full time. Meant leaving Stirling.

A move to Perth was planned. Perth, a city at that point in my tiny mind only known for its outstanding swimming pool, river rapids and post swim chips.

I will never forget the days when both Ash and I were young, not long after dad married Morag; that her brother Donnie very kindly took Ash and me to Perth leisure pool on Sundays. He has a daughter, Jody, ages with us and what a joyous adventure that used to be. I really enjoyed those times. The excitement of being swooped up in the rapid water and swished down a conveyor belt of chlorine-infested water was for a dull moment never to be had. I sometimes wish I were 11 again.

So yes Perth. Scoped out over the coming weeks as my new home. Very quickly realizing I had an ability to negotiate essentials I needed without costing me too much. Took out a new credit card. Got myself a cheeky flat. HOME. Home away from home. First time I was to live alone. Not a care in the world. Who knew!! I had an ability to act and think like an adult.

I had THE smallest TV known to man. This little yellow number from the downstairs entertainment section of Debenhams that mum scored a tidy discount in at that time. (Remember this is early 2002). That TV, sitting on the biggest shelf in this huge flat I am renting, with its shady sofas, old school non-modern approach to decor was my whole world.

Could I cook? Nope.

Could I survive alone? Jury was out.

Could I clean? Yes. Arguably, though upon exit of said flat one year later that was not the verdict of the jury. Eww. HA.

My first night I ate a whole 3 by 9 milky bar. You know the size I mean. There really is no other way to describe the larger than you normally buy, but not family of four size chocolate bar. That. In around 3 minutes. I took solace in knowing chocolate was my company. For I sure as hell did not feel it coming from this huge flat filled with THE smallest TV known to humanity. Had my box sets, a cheeky VCR and a six quid Argos lamp though so my fears quickly disintegrated. I was flying solo. For the first time in my early adulthood, I was to live alone. Bills were my responsibility and maturity set upon me demanding my full attention like a tramp on chips at midnight.

Council tax though. If I may just touch upon the sheer audacity of the charges. In those days I was astounded. You know that more than 10% of my monthly income, which at this point is a mere 800 a month; council tax was 90 quid and I was a single person. Honest to God I felt like I was being bent over every month just for the sheer liberty of gracing Perth's sleepy hollow with my central belt existence. But the fact that TK Max was a mere stones throw from my flat was music to my ears. At that point, my favorite band was Linkin Park. "And in the end it doesn't even matter". Never truer words spoken. So TK max was my monthly fix. A little purchase now and then never hurt anyone. And if Linking Park said so then it was all good. When they collaborated with Jay Z, my mind was blown. Speaking of Jay Z why does he not age? He has looked 25 since like 1995. I need me some of that anti-ageing cream.

Soon met a whole world of new people from all over the northern part of Scotland. Amazing time, it really was. People who I cherish to this day, some gone, some still around and some I would rather forget. But life is full of times sent to try us. And boy did my time in Perth try me.

If it was not the ridiculous uniform bestowed on me, it was my inability to curb my spending. I had very quickly and actually surprisingly forgotten about my obsession with starving myself. I had replaced that fixation with spending. On things, I did not need. But a cool pair of Jeans from Top Shop were a necessity right? Wrong. Within a few months, I had racked up 3k on my credit card. At that point, with around 60 pounds spare on my credit card for spending (I know I know SHAMEFUL), this was the time that the joy that is GHD Hair straighteners made their way on to the "scene". I can honestly say I remember that day as if it was yesterday.

My hair. A complete frizz bomb of extremism was in dire need of calming down. These babies came onto the market and studies were rife. Word of mouth spread like the legs of a call girl that these were the must have item of that decade. Like ever. Could I afford them? No. Because I was sporting a wardrobe full of TK Max, clothes my Nana would have been proud of but that I actually never even wore. So my hair was a riot but at least I convinced myself I was a trendy little cookie.

You will never guess the risk I took next. Ok, you probably will. I do protest though, that it was completely unlike me to act with such carelessness and rascal like tendencies.

I only went and bough the GHD's and maxed out my card and went OVER my limit. *monkey face*

My hair was like a horses' mane. Beautiful, shiny and straight and I felt like a million dollars. I will never forget the feeling of looking at them when I got them home and out of the box as if they were gold in my hands. They were like my new best friend. The ultimate accessory to someone of my age that time. If I could relate it to anything now it would be a smart phone. Never leaving home without it. Except in this instance, it was more the service it provided. Unbelievable hair. That could last days. But remember these are the days' dry shampoo was but a long overdue idea in my eyes.

My hair was straight all the time. My belly was slowly becoming curvy again though. *double monkey face*. But I often ask myself when reminiscing was I underneath it all happier then than I had ever been? Was I maturing into a more accepting adult than the self-loathing prophecy I had allowed myself to become in recent years? Could it all be because I was learning to accept responsibility for everything that went right and wrong in my life? Yes. It was in my eyes at that time all because of my newfound social vortex. My world of completeness was fulfilling and enlightening and it was all to become a whole lot better.

I was much unprepared for the feelings of joy, love and contentment I found with some new friends I made in Perth. Having shared part time employer with some and a full time employer with others, I really did feel like I was able to suppress my anxiety a little by just saying yes to kind invites to do things. Like go out, go bowling, go to the cinema and just live. Without care or worry.

I became very close to two people in Perth, both of whom worked part time in the bar I worked in. Fiona and Stephen. They brought a sense of fun and 'live in the moment' mantra to our interactions. I really thrived in their presence.

We did everything together. Them more so as a duo as they lived together in what I can only describe as a fucking castle. They rented this huge open plan 2 story townhouse with the most amazing setting overlooking Perth's Inch and the bridge. Was something quite spectacular. Although I did often wonder how they afforded the electricity bill as it was so big! However, we took real pleasure in throwing the coolest parties there.

It was in that house, soon to be known as the "Chateau", that we discovered our shared appreciation of the film Scary Movie 2. An utterly hilarious spoof comedy by the Wayans brothers. The quotes we used from that film occupied 90% of our conversation thereafter and still do. When I see Fiona now we manage to always find ourselves in a scenario, any scenario, it might be we just be passing a bus stop and boom a quote comes to life. It is what defines our friendship I feel. The lyrics "shake yo ass watch yourself" are often our opening lines to each other. And we can go months of not even speaking.

Not to mention Stephens daily doggy bag from Pizza Hut. I had a car so Fiona and I would regularly pick Stephen up from work at around 10pm and he would no doubt appear from the entrance with about five pizza boxes of leftovers. Fat club was always mortifying on a Thursday because I was always gaining. Fatty. Pizza cheesy fatty. How 3 reasonably sane humans could consume ALL the leftovers having had dinner a mere 3 hours before every late shift he did was a beyond me. They were both skinnies. It was just me turning into a pizza.

And so as my derriere got bigger, so did my spending habits. On clothes. What is it about women and buying clothes?

My new straight hair was an utter joy though. I had zero style but straight hair and in those days of no filter, no Facebook, no cyber interaction, straight hair was THE number one fashion accessory. In addition, everyone who was anyone in show business (Perth!) had GHD straighteners.

I had not yet discovered how to contour though. Let us not get too carried away. I am only

20 at this point...That took another 11 years to set its sights on my ageing youth.

I think I had and still have quite an old soul. I used to believe I was the reincarnation of an old unmarried woman cat lady in my previous life. Whilst walking to work in Perth I would often talk to any animal I would see. Like a modern day mentally unstable Alice in Wonderland. Except this was Melanie in Perthland...

The Dunkeld Mile. A multitude of desperate sales pushing car dealerships where I was to purchase my new green Punto. Having had my first ever car, my white micra, written off as an insurance companies worst nightmare after a horrible accident.

May 11th 2001, a desperately horrific night. A journey home with only minutes to reach my doorstep and a huge lorry misinterprets the road signals and ploughs straight into the back of my small hatchback. Removing me a good 100 ft. into the central reservation as I waited patiently at a roundabout giving way to oncoming traffic. The memory of that impact will never leave my mind. The fear for my passengers, the fear for my car and the fear for my injured neck catapulted from the pits of my stomach to my head like a bolt of lightning. What had happened? And how was I going to fix it?

Had not clocked my insurance was third party had I. No sirree.

Had not appreciated that I DID have legal cover though and what do you know, the driver of the lorry was not insured and was a foreigner. So the European court of human rights was to be the centric institution that would be to handle my lawsuit for damages over the coming 4 years. For I had an injury, a car that was written off beyond possibility of repair and a bank balance that would not actually allow me to pay to fix the car completely. And it needed it. Badly.

Therefore, I traded it in. For the green Punto. S reg. Boy did it smell good. There are very little things in life that produce the smug look and feeling you have driving off in a new car. Albeit it was second hand. It was my only hand. And I loved it. Good riddance to the car that nearly killed me.

I should point out my passengers were all fine. Just me that was so rudely injured and suitably entered into a long drawn out legal war with European insurance bureaus – which was kindly carried out by Direct Line Legal department on my behalf – best 20 pounds ever spent. However, it did take around 254 years. Honestly. For what? For 4000 pounds, that is what! HOORAY. More on that later…

So I've a new Punto, an injury claims under way, some decent friends in Perth, a full time job that seen me sell gas and electricity over the phone which was ironically really quite cool. Ever so nervous taking my first call though. But I very quickly became a diva on that welcome line.

9

Friars funhouse

Living away from home for the first time was a liberating experience for sure. I very quickly grew in maturity and tolerance for my own mistakes. I never knew how to cook properly or how to diet properly but I always ate. I never knew how to clean a house properly but I always had air freshener and I never really understood the importance of valuing my income until it sneaked up on me that my credit card was maxed and al I had to show for it for straight hair and a bigger arse.

So, along came the summer of 2003. The summer of Sean Paul and Blu Cantrell. Friends Season 9. BBQ's a plenty. My 21st birthday celebration planning. The nightclub dancers and their libidos AND me meeting someone very special indeed…

My best friend Sam; friends since 2001, when it transpired we shared the same surname and thus obviously we had to become friends. So yes, Sam, had been studying in Stirling but working p/t in Perth alongside myself, Fiona and Stephen and so on weekends stayed at my flat.

When it became apparent we wanted to live together, the quest to find somewhere to live, in Stirling, was an adventure for us both. I personally got a rather too excited that a friend wanted to live with me and took the planning to the extremes. She is still friends with me so I must be doing something right. I like to think we are kindred spirits.

Therefore, the plan was that I would pack up my 1 year of living in Perth, Sam would pack up her halls of residence contents from the University of Stirling, and we would trot off into the sunset together. To Stirling. To Friars Street. To the Top floor of a block of trendy flats situated on the walkway from the Bars at the top of the pedestrian walk way right to the bottom. Therefore, you can imagine the noise all weekend. Joy oh fucking joy.

We found this cool flat. Two bed, huge living room, tiny kitchen and questionable heating. Nevertheless, it was modern and the proprietors owned the restaurant downstairs so chips on tap were a go-go. There were arguably 96 floors to climb to get to the door but it was a nice pad and we sure did get excited signing the lease. Six months.

It came with most furnishings so many of my acquired Perth flat contents had to be sold/given to charity/given to my sister. Packing up my Perth flat was nostalgic as it came with so many memories of the times I had there.

There is certainly something to be said for finding old photographs, receipts, condom wrappers, clothes bought 10 months previously with tags intact and a credit card statement with the big red letters IN ARREARS! Shit the bed the time was now for growing up!

And so, 24 black bags later the Hammerman Buildings flat was packed, the property owner had released my 200 pounds' deposit, much to his demise considering I had painted the lounge a horrific midnight blue one night whilst watching the Blair witch project. Who actually does that!

Anyway. Locked the doors and said goodbye.

Friar street funhouse was to be our new home. And so, we moved in. Early May 2003. Right when the Black Eyed Peas released "Where is the Love?" We had quite a few of everything so we decided to hold a car boot sale. Sam and I. At crack of dawn on a Sunday having both done a night shift in one of the nightclub venues we worked for. That was dedication to the cause if ever there was one. Happy girls we were not. Holy shitballs. We had to drag our asses down to Kildean market car boot and set up home for all the bargain hunters to accost your goods like a junkie on crack. "Have you goat any jewelry hen?" "I am not even out the car yet pal give me 5 minutes" – Jesus. H. Christ. It was like vultures' day out.

I had no jewelry. But what I did have was the finest Ikea crockery, shoes, clothes, a multitude of jackets (in all sizes!), banter, a large coffee and a mood on me like no other. But we each walked away with 60 odd quid and that was a glorious amount to be earning in those days. Remember it is 2003 and a Twix still costs less than 50p.

What did we do with said 60 pounds you may so rightly ask? At age 20, almost 21 it is astounding that we would not automatically save now is not? YES! We took ourselves to the bar down the bottom of the road and got absolutely smashed on a Sunday night. There really was no need but we were greedy student/poor workers living in poverty who needed a dance.

Not to mention we are living in denial that there is no central heating system in the beauty of a flat we reside in! Nothing. Therefore, we decided to have a conversation with the owner…

"We can get you a gas heater".

"Aye ok".

Stunk to high heaven but generated heat like nothing else. And boy did we appreciate that.

What I have failed to mention is that at no point upon viewing this soon-to-be-our-home had we thought to question the heating. And Sam was a university scholar no less!!

Having moved in during the summer it was highly convenient that it was not necessarily that cold that we noticed the lack of heating but boy were the coming months soon to surprise me into secretly turning the oven on and keeping the door open! Sam went mental. I needed heat though. It was a tough time.

That summer was real fun. Real. Real fun. We spent a lot of time together Sam and me. So much so, we became so close and we still are. Michael, her boyfriend was a regular visitor and was like part of the house family. It was lovely living with her. We did not have the same eating tastes as by this point I was quite the fast food, unhealthy, convenient meal hound dog and she was a healthy little poppet. Still is. As am I but it was amazing how different we were personally but how in harmony we were as friends. We went out together, we shared cars, banter, memories I will cherish.

I am certain it was her obsessive yet adorable compulsion for cleanliness and keeping a "tidy house" for I have lived like a control freak ever since.

We spent our first Christmas in that flat. Right around the months that Pop Idol seen Michelle McManus win first place and sweep the nations hearts with her incredible voice. We used to spend Saturday nights getting ready for our respective pub shifts by sitting on the edge of our black sofa watching Pop Idol and straightening our hair in front of the huge mirror. Remember we are obsessed with GHD's. It was as if every female's hair had developed an addiction to the seductive heat of the hair irons. A-maze-ing. Capital A.

Matched with our Nokia 3210's and Snake II we really felt we were as cool as school. Sense the irony.

Location wise it was convenient living there. What was not convenient was parking. On a pedestrian precinct where drunken fools regularly attempt to roll dive your car. And one night they succeeded. So I wake up one morning for work. For the long ass journey up the motorway to Perth in my green Punto and there is a note on my windscreen underneath my window wipers. "Please call Central Scotland Police". And of course, I was initially thinking shit this is me being done for parking illegally for like 6 months and now they have had enough. Life over. That, or Sam called them and reported that she was about to murder her flat mate (me) for having that bloody oven open and on 6 hours a night just to get a heat. Mr. Charming Police Officer was actually very friendly. I remember visiting him the following Sunday at Police HQ to discuss.

It transpired that someone had taken a swan dive onto my bonnet, up onto my roof, opened their belt, pulled down their zipper, revealed their penis and urinated all over my roof. All the while being filmed by CCTV, waving at patrons who stood in awe, watching, laughing and waiting for the grand finale; a somersault off the roof, down off the car, pulling his trousers up and making his way to the chip shop for a fish supper…

I know what you are thinking. He did not even wash his hands. How disgusting. Hilarious.

So my poor car is there bare, abused and riddled in drunken urine afforded to her by some drunken ass punk who forgot he was being filmed.

However, it was that fateful Sunday I went to make my statement and met Mr. Charming. The Police Officer with the golden smile. God bless his approach to trying to explain why they had called me in. They had arrested him for drunk and disorderly, shown him the footage and advised him that they would contact the owner of the car (me) to check if I wanted to press charges. Now initially I questioned the charge. Because in my mind, there was not actually any physical damage. I had subsequently treated Poppy Punto to a deluxe valet and scrub a dub dub wash at the local Jet fuel station. However, upon asking for a quick5 minute recess giving my statement I went and further inspected my car. What do you know; I had a huge dent on the roof? So charges were filed. Mr. 'I piss all over people's car roofs and cause damage with my attempt at aerobatics' had damaged my car and I was damned if he was not going to foot the bill to repair her. And repair her he did. He was ordered to pay me every month for a whole year and of course that Punto never seen a cent of the money. She was traded in for a flashy brand spanking new Blue Punto, only 2 years old. This was only when I finally secured a job working in the banking industry.

Let me take you back just slightly to my interest in banking. I had developed a real interest in the corporate office, 9-5 lifestyle Dolly Parton so eloquently chanted about but also acted to finesse in the film of the same name. I longed to find a long-term goal and career interest that would see me do something with my brains. I might not have been the academic scholar I had really hoped I had the determination and capacity to achieve; but I certainly did have the desire to fulfil some sort of routine. Go to work, work hard, receive a paycheck, and make my parents proud.

I made an appointment to speak to the branch manager of our local TSB. I had met him once before when visiting the branch with my mum. I did not really know what went on in a bank but I did know if I was going to make something of my life, this was my chance. To make a good first impression, show my interest in working for the banking industry, ask for advice and see if he could help me. Bearing in mind to date I had only managed to accomplish full time bar work, voice work for a directory enquiry service and selling gas and electricity to the public. Of course all of which paid a bill. But none of which filled a void I had been feeding and muting since I knew what emotion was. So this was my chance.

His name was Mr. Wylie. A charming manager. He was smart and professional. I was a nervous wreck. I stood outside waiting for my appointment. Appointment of course that implied I was just another customer looking for help with my personal account. Nothing to do with trying to find work. But my name was called and in I went.

"Hello, my name is Melanie Hume, I am 21, I live locally and bank with TSB and I would like to work in this branch. I am not sure what function I have the skills or capacity to fulfil but I am a fast learner and I would really love an opportunity to join this bank."

"Hello Melanie, I am Mr. Wylie, the Branch Manager. I would love to help you. Do you have your CV he said? "Yes of course" I said. And we exchanged a mutual appreciation for my candor and my belief and hope bestowed onto him that he could potentially change my life. And change the course of my professional life from "working a job" to "embarking on a career" was something he deserves full credit for. Of course, I played a part with my dazzling smile, but everybody loves a story eh…

And so, I left the branch that day feeling elated. I did not have a new job quite yet. No no, I was still travelling up and down that horrific motorway to Perth to cold call people who had seen the light and joined another gas company. I was earning a pittance, but still worshipping the fact I was back living in my hometown, getting to enjoy my mums cooking at least twice a week.

It was not for a further 8 weeks of misery, that Christmas came and went and I had lost all hope that TSB did not have an interest in hiring me. I still had no further knowledge in knowing how one would become a member of the banking world. I did not even know anything about call centers at this stage either. Everything out with university, retail, nightlife bar work and gas and electric was a complete mystery. It is any wonder I survived. I barely knew how to boil an egg. I still did not at age 30!

Anyway, January 2004 was a cold cold month. One of the coldest. Bitterly freezing temperatures meant that starting the car in the morning was tough and my S reg green Punto was showing real signs of deterioration. I was convinced the trauma of having harry no pants peeing on her sleeping one night truly affected her ability to go on. Therefore, I had to make the decision to take a bank loan and upgrade.

The first week in February, I received a call. A call from TSB bank HQ asking me to interview for a position of Personal Banking Manager. Oh my actual god. The man done me proud. I was to attend an interview at the Hilton in Glasgow a mere few days later and the nerves hit me like a bull in a china shop. I think up until that moment I had only been that excited when my dad advised he was marrying Morag.

This might be a career for me. Gosh, I desperately desired to be something. To make something out of my life. I felt so disappointed in myself that not all I had achieved until this date was actually worth mentioning or feeling proud about. I genuinely had one of those poker face smiles that are the life and soul but deep down I longed for something more meaningful. Therefore, I researched TSB, their code of conduct, their mission statement, their board, their hierarchy, structure, products, services and branch locations. I knew that there was a chance I would be working in Stirling. My hometown, my home branch. With colleagues that had opened my account when I was 11. It was a belly warming feeling.

I approached my interview with a hole in my trousers but a fire in my belly. My interviewer, Anna, was a certified TSB trainer and was based in the central region area for TSB. She was looking for two staff, one for Stirling or Falkirk and one for Irvine or Hamilton branches. I gave it my best shot. I opted for honesty. I told her why I left university having not completed my second year; why I opted for bar work over a degree; life selling gas and electric over a more sustainable long-term career of which I had no knowledge of, and generally believed that banking was to be my future. I offered my raw self and told her she would not find anyone more proud to say I worked for TSB. My bank.

Unfortunately, the job description they so eloquently detailed in such depth did not quite register with my passion, interests or indeed skills, but I was not one to turn my back to an excellent opportunity. If they believed in me. I believed in me. And that day I felt alive. Truly alive for the first time in years. I had the shittiest quality trousers on but boy did I feel worthy of a corporate workplace whose goals, people, grandeur resonated in my soul. And so I was dismissed, thanked for my time and told I would hear in a matter of weeks…

That joyous day came. One-day sitting in the canteen of my existing workplace. I am eating a sandwich and a call comes from HR department at TSB.

"Miss Hume, Melanie Hume"

"Yes, speaking"

"We are calling from TSB and are delighted to verbally offer you the position of Personal Banking Manager at our Stirling Branch"

Stands in motion jumping up and down fisting the air and thinking happy thoughts

"Stirling branch really?"

"Yes Melanie, we would like you to start as soon as possible. You will attend training for 1 month, learning our products, processes and meeting the team and then you will have your own portfolio of clients which you will acquire from the existing manager who is moving on".

Oh. My. God. I was thrilled. I lived a mere 5-minute walk from the Stirling branch. I was so excited that I had a real job, career, future to look forward to and a salary of 15K to accompany it. In early 2004 that was a lot for a 21-year-old university drop out. Or so I believed. I was utterly overjoyed that they believed in me. Something I said must have resonated and I managed to feel some inner confidence at my ability to do something good for my life. I felt proud of me. Proud for me. Proud to tell me Dad.

Resignation submitted. The immense pleasure that I took in knowing that I did not need to fund 40 pounds a week in fuel any longer was excitement in itself that things were looking up. I would have a little more money, less travel, what I thought would be a flourishing profession and a new start at my working life.

So my final weeks in Perth were on the countdown. I had made some great friends up there. One in particular…Leah Williams. What a gem she was. We had a mutual interest in anything funny, anything sinister and the banter flowed daily. She lit up our working day and I thrived knowing she was around. What an absolute laugh we had on that Welcome line. There were a few others who contributed to some cool memories but the sendoff was really quite sweet. Finished off with a night out in the local haunts of Perth high street and an overnight stay with Tracey was to contribute to my delightful farewell hangover.

The journey back to Stirling the following morning was one of nostalgia. I felt like I was saying my final goodbye to Perth. To the memories of nightlife, energy knowledge, parties on the Dunkeld Road, TK Maxx, Living Well Gym, the nights I broke down a stone's throw from the fuel station, Stephens pizza parties, the "Chateau", the dodgy parking habits I acquired AND the friends I made for a lifetime but never to see regularly anymore. Goodbye to Perth. A continuing hello to my swanky apartment in Friar Street, where the heat came to die.

The drive back to Stirling was actually longer than usual because of course it was pissing rain and with potholes a plenty, the traffic was slower than a tortoise raise. However, upon arrival at Friar Street I felt elated. We simply had to celebrate. But I was working that night goddamit and so was Sam! So we both prepared for our respective night shifts and made our way to our clubs for our nights of servicing the happy public. However, it was quiet and I was released early so I decided to go out and joyously celebrate my pending jail sentence with TSB. I use the term jail sentence flippantly as a way of sarcasm of giving up my rather "bum type" lifestyle for you know, a proper job, when in reality I was so excited I nearly peed my pants on many occasions counting down the days. BUT, little did I actually know working for that company for the long, drawn out painful year, in the company of one of the most narcissistic, overbearing arrogant women I have ever met; it was like spending a year in Cornton Vale. Scotland's only women's Prison. Horrific times were upon me...

Monday morning. Friar street sunshine beaming through my top floor window, the birds were chirping, I had a lovely new uniform to don, I had my car fueled and I was ready for my first day working for TSB. Trustee Savings Banks. One of the top banks in the UK. I was going to be a somebody. I travelled to Falkirk, parked at Pets at Home because parking was horrendous and trotted on up to their headquarters to meet Teresa, the Regional Trainer, and lovely girl. Very well to do and polite. And Neil. The other PBM who would be assigned to Hamilton. He was pleasant too. The niceties out the way, it was time to get down to business. We were thrown royally in at the deep end. Given brochures, literature, buddies to watch and learn from, a PC to look at client data was all too overwhelming, and may I say badly structured for a training program. I still however excelled in column marked "excited". I felt so corporate. Surrounded by established and experienced bankers, one of which was a tall Financial Planner called Frank. He was super funny. I felt like I was at some sort of boot camp. It was only on day 1, at around 2pm that the stark reality of the Personal Banking Managers "targets" and "sales expected per quarter" really highlighted just how demanding the role would eventually be to me. For me. And against me. Fun times on Friar Street were about to come to an abrupt end.

10

An emotional shift

The spring had sprung. In both 2004 and in the item of furniture I called bed at the Fun factory or Friar Street!

I could not figure out if it was attention and recognition I yearned for yet surely working for a bank would demand that? I just wanted to feel that, should there be an apparent matrix of how you are ranked in terms of value in comparison to people who made your life hell growing up; that I ranked number 1. It was like a victorious salute of fuck you, you and you, simmered under my slight introverted demeanor. A job in a bank was never going to require an IQ of 200, but to me, at that particular date, time and era of my existence, it encouraged a feeling in me of wanting and desiring to be viewed as better. Precisely better than what was never a question I asked myself. I just used that adjective to describe the feeling. I was doing better. I had a better than before income but did I feel more confident in myself? Not really. Did my many years of disliking me disappear? No.

If I am honest, I had always been one for the limelight. Loving attention. From anyone. Ironically, the attention I attracted in my younger years through Primary and into early Secondary had not been what I wanted or indeed deserve. No one deserves that. But having been a child without a mother for some time before Morag came along I tried to place a lot of the background reasoning to my yearning interest in me, on the fact I had gone "without" something instinctively I perhaps needed. Not that I have ever classed that "loss" as love. Because my dad loved me, so much I do not have any negative memories. Albeit nostalgic and gut wrenching to think of some of those lonely nights crying in bed and wanting my dad to cuddle me for whatever reason, and those memories draw a tear; the epitome of childhood is having memories. To look back on and smile, even the sound of his name brings me back to me. Not ever forgetting that those nights I lay crying, he too was sad and next-door.

Attention, for me, I think looking back at my younger years and thus the importance of that "all eyes on me" desire I had acquired by my 22nd year was really about acceptance.

Acceptance. Such a profound word. Acceptance.

"Acceptance in human psychology is a person's assent to the reality of a situation, a process or condition (often a negative or uncomfortable situation) without attempting to change it, or protest" (Reference: Wikipedia).

I have often found my neurotic nature of wanting calm, everything tidy and in order, lack of patience and irritated opinion of things not going according to how my mind works to be a result of my wanting acceptance. Wanting my thoughts, dreams, sorrows and woes to be heard. Therefore, the physical behaviors' I displayed were in my opinion my subconscious' way of controlling and accepting me. Wasn't that the first hurdle? To accept myself as I was? I think so. Guilt was ever so apparent though whilst exhibiting my need to be noticed. Almost desperation for compliments to follow me around and boost my faltering ego. How sad is that? To be so pathetic in ones' self to only thrive of fellow humans' attempt at boosting your ego. Whether it is the actual truth or not. Who cared? I did not. I had lost all sense of knowing how to distinguish between deceit and authentic behaviors of others. I convinced myself only my work place, my new harmonious surroundings were the only playing field for my neurosis to truly feel at home. Obviously, this feeling of being incapable of knowing how truly people feel about you was not news to me. Nor is it a historical sentiment as I write this biography at age 30-something. It is ever apparent in anyone that I understand. However, for a person of deep inner turmoil, with no root conscious knowing or reasoning, it is certainly a feeling that quantifies in size whilst breeding in a small area within your mind. In other words 'the cortex home to emotions', according to google that is. LOL.

Sounds rather sad and almost frustrating to read of such a pitiful tale. I completely agree with any ready at this stage thinking "oh for fuck sake Mel, man up".

I agree.

Wholeheartedly. I really wish I had the ability at that stage to shake myself, know I had a roof over my head, a car, a job, friends, food on the table, condoms in my drawer and a nightclub a stones' throw from my flat. Sure, a girl should have been delighted with life. Ironically, I was elated. On the surface, I was grinning ear to ear. Loving the fact, I felt 'better' than those who I thought were less fortunate but guilty that I felt that way. Almost as if I felt bad for feeling like I deserved something. For a change, I wanted to feel no sorrow but the guilt ate away at my conscience for feeling smug about anything in my life. This was never the intention. To feel I benefited from anyone's or anything else's misfortune. To just have a moment of solidarity and retribution from my reckless and turmoil disposition was a joy failing to behold itself upon me ever. I desperately wanted it to vacate my mind and allow me the freedom to rejoice in finding positivity. I learned the correct word for my guilt overcoming the smug approach, humility. Anyone exerting humility in anything in life should of course continue to do so. It is a sad fact that reality in todays' generation can be lost in translation or just lost completely. That is not to say that every single human being has an element of selfishness embedded in his or her being.

So gradually, the "being better" mantra diminished. Replaced by feelings of awe. In awe of learning a new skill in banking, learning to just take day by day, living with friends, working a night job in a bar and generally doing what 20 something girls did. Live. Why was I so tough on myself though? Always feeling insignificant. Like what I had to offer was just simply not enough. Or so that was the case according to my own mind. Looking back, it never was that way in actual reality. This was my paranoia. Like a grumbling anxiety that I am the victim of rejection in all walks of life and yet I had so many materialistic things to be ever so thankful and grateful for.

Unfortunately, my employer's choice of colleagues left me feeling bullied yet again. An incessant narcissistic fellow Account manager was nothing short of exhausting. To be around, to hear about, to listen to, to be lectured by, to be beaten by in terms of targets and not once did she teach me anything. She did make it in to my book though so I am going to credit her with an encouragement that contributed to me becoming confidant enough to walk away from that salary, job title, credibility in such a huge organization.

To another bank. A bigger bank. The world's best bank at that time, 2005. To less money, to what I presumed would be a different type of sell. Telephony once again. However, my gut instinct told me the 45-minute commute; 6-week training, reduction in salary would be the right move for me. And right move it was.

January 2005 seen me feel part of a team once again. Selling bank products over the telephone was tough. Training was tough but the "academy" time was 6 weeks I will remember fondly. My coaches were helpful, the hours were reasonable, the people were nice and I made some friends. The immense pressure of retail banking with TSB had vacated the space it had rented for a long 9 months in my head and on my shoulders. Looking back, I think the structure of training and development for new starts at my new job gave me peace internally that everything had a plan and boy, I loved a plan. Amazing how neurotic one can be about detail and knowledge of plans. I guess it was something that my training with TSB has seriously lacked for me personally. Or perhaps I just was not built for face-to-face sales?! After all, I loved to spend money so I was hardly the pillar of sense. Actual hilarious.

And so training was complete and it was time to set us recruits free on society. God help the public.

But the public I helped. I smashed my first months targets; I enjoyed chatting about the banks products. I had undoubtedly the best self-made manual on all things information relevant for discussing with clients over the phone. It was liberating. However, with all things wonderful comes a shitty shift pattern. Honestly the week of 2-10pm shifts over the weekends was utterly soul destroying. Sat on my arse for 8 hours on a Saturday made me want to claw my eyes out.

I do remember one day though I got a call from our home insurance company who were paying us 756 quid to replace our sofa. The sofa I had managed to get black hair dye all over. Accidentally...

Black and shiny hair. And not a single grey hair at that age! Joyous. Bloody surprising after the shit I stomached the previous year. Including a brief spell of fainting in work. Joy to the world that was. Not.

Bought ourselves a new sofa. A huge gigantic sofa built for about 35 people! It was utterly amazing. Salesman managed to flog us the warranty and some pointless cover should it ever be damaged. But of course, I had a cat. Toby. Toby and his 10 claws of wonder.

Toby. Toby came into my life thanks to a girl I met a couple of years before, circa. 2001, March. A girl who will always be a friend to me. We shared some good times. Pamela. Pammie.

I firmly believe some of the happiest days of my life were with her by my side. Pamela and Mel. Coated in yesterdays' make up doing our housework on a Saturday in our fresh pajamas from Primark. Loving life. Always laughing at each other's jokes. We were so close. So in harmony with each other it was heartwarming to have someone other than a loved one finish my sentences because we just knew what each other were thinking. All the livelong day.

She brought Toby to me. For my birthday. For my 23rd birthday she wrapped up his food tray, food bowl, "a guide to looking after your new kitten", a lip-gloss and his carrier individually and left him waiting in the hallway. All the while, she duped me into thinking she was coming over with the Indian takeaway we always had. A chicken chasni. With rice, pakora and naan bread. It makes me salivate thinking of it. So yummy. Not the cat, the chasni…

So there I am sitting stunned at these random gifts and I have yet to see a kitten…

Until, the lounge door of my flat in Camelon is opened and in comes the smallest black and white poppet. Little darling. Light of my life. I immediately loved every hair on his tiny body. I lifted him up and could have eaten him I adored every little meow he mustered in his early years. He was a mere 12 weeks old. No name. I had pondered on Puchi. What the fuck was wrong with me? No one knew. Then I had an epiphany. Toby was to be his name and it fitted him perfectly. He immediately shits all over my cream carpet. I loved him more. Wrapping him in a blanket like a tiny baby was the only thing maternally I felt I needed to do. Even though cats obviously hate that shit. Ha. Was it a match made in heaven? I utterly adored him. He was cute as a button. I am sure I irritated the shit out of him with my incessant need for affection from him. I was forever lifting him and he looked at me regularly as if I had urinated in his tuna. I had not. Who would! Needless to say I just loved having him near me.

We had a bed that was metal in frame. The frame had sections that you could access from beneath the bed and Toby would regularly wake us by jumping at our feet as they poked through the bed covers. That was painful as Satan himself sculpted his claws but I still never found it in me to shout at him. He was my boy. I actually think that at times I enjoyed conversation with him more than Mark, my boyfriend.

It is amazing how pets completely influence your life. Everything we did from then on in had an impact on Toby. Holidays, nights out, letting him outside and even the weekly shop. I always sneaked him tuna and whipped cream when Mark was not looking which royally fattened him up. I cannot express how much I miss Toby thinking back now that he is at his forever home with my friend Laura. She kindly took him when I moved to Abu Dhabi.

No animal lover will ever say they do not talk to their pets. If they are not in regular conversation, it is not a pet; it is an ornament. Toby knew. He just knew. Sometimes he would act like a teenager and sulk and other times he would relish in testing my patience when changing the bed sheets BUT his presence gave me a real sense of home.

I think having some companionship, a steady income in a job I liked, albeit telesales and I could have challenged myself more, I had become quite settled. Perhaps that was what I had always looked for? To just feel settled. Perhaps turmoil and anxiety had rented space in my soul for just a bit too long? My Toby was the light of my life.

It is only fitting and fair to touch on the memory of my time with Mark. He was my very first love. Brought together through sheer chance. Mentioning him will be without any tongue and cheek humor. A first you say? Yes, well it was no laughing matter.

Meeting Mark changed me. It made me feel wanted. We had a friendship before we had a relationship and to this day, I stand by the notion that a friendship prior to romance can and sometimes always contributes to solidifying the foundations of something great. Whilst Mark was unfortunately struggling with a difficult relationship break up, I could not help my feelings for him. In typical twenty something fashion though, our first encounter was because of a drink too many. Nevertheless, contrary to the "one night stands don't a relationship make" myth; we dodged the sceptic bullets a plenty and tried to fight the need and desire to be together but could not. So much so that my heart felt like it was on fire. I had allowed a fragment of my interior wall to disintegrate and let someone touch me. He had a good heart and was a good person. He made mistakes but he had a quality I had not experienced before in meeting someone romantically and I could sit here all day listing the reasons why I wondered what he seen in little old me but that would be rather self-destructive. The truth is I did not experience worry or anxiety because I laid it all bare. Our first encounter he seen it all so I had nothing physically to use as a bargaining tool.

We spent nights together, we watched pulp fiction together, we ate ice cream together, we took road trips together, he helped me upgrade my green Punto to a shiny new blue Punto AND he introduced me to his mum. We were *friends*. Moreover, lovers who were growing into something more unified.

Some would say we moved very quickly. In addition to being a lot older and wiser nowadays, I would advise my younger self to slow down. However, when you know you know. Love cannot wait. It is the only emotion that cannot be tailored or taught to react to demands. Love is like a powerful tool that rules supreme over all the strength your body and mind is capable of handling. I really did love him. He helped me love myself. He offered me a drawer in his clothes dresser one day and his heart the next. It was a special time. I used to refer to him as my little sea horse. His touch, his hugs, his kisses and his general presence made me feel so liberated at life. All whilst I hated my time at TSB it was joyous knowing I was going home to Mark every night and we had Sky TV. That is a big deal.

In essence, my love for him was a love letter coming to life. He was my family. My family loved him. I loved him. I will always look back on our memories fondly. Relationships of course do not come without tough times and tough times we had however he was committed and so was I.

We took some special trips as a couple and of which were before the days of the selfie, the "check-in", the filter and the smart phone. For us it was a disposable camera, factor 50 and a promise of a postcard that took us on vacation.

Funny when I think back now to those mid-noughties when smart phones had not even been invented yet. What did we do with our time? Life. We did life. With no filter. Except

I did have a little filter. My grannie pants from M&S were always at hand to keep me feeling cozy.

Therefore, the popular things of 2005 and 2006 were of course One Tree Hill, my favorite program! Colored contact lenses, halter neck tops and small boutique style hand bags. Of which I was incessantly buying all the time on eBay!

This leads me to the purchase of all purchases. Now it takes a keen bidder and a rather bored person to trail the eBay site looking for bargains *but* the decision to take a trip. The trip of all trips. A trip that would require us to really make the most of our time...

In Chicago. Chicago, a beautiful city. A windy city. In the March of 2006, Mark and I decided to put our unique interest in WWE (yes the Wrestling!) to the test. We decided we would go to WrestleMania. Every couple does that right? Right? No?

For any reader who does not know what the WWE are. Think Hulk Hogan. You are welcome.

So I sourced us flights, accommodation AND TICKETS! To WrestleMania. On eBay. The grandest tool of all. On the WWW you understand. Online, via a really dated PC that took about a year to load up and then dial up to the Wi-Fi. Those were the days.

The day of jaunting to Chicago arrived. I have packed arguably the biggest bag known to humanity. Being so assured that it would be cold and less touristy, more adventure, we wanted to be prepared. We were not prepared for the horrendous journey to London and then out to Chicago with British Airways but the service was ok. I am certain Mark and I raided the in-flight mini-bar to the point they gave us that look...you know that look "don't start your shit with us". Such a fun memory.

The feeling when we arrived was joyous. I was that excited I was filled with emotion. I could not believe we were actually going to attend the most entertaining show on earth. Do not get me wrong most people thought we were weird having an interest in the wrestling but having been a huge fan since I was about 10, this was a dream come true even at my mature age of 24/25 going on seven!

We had secured tickets for the Hall of Fame; a ceremony only 300 fans go to. A ceremony where stars, fighters, retired wrestlers are inducted in the WWE Hall of Fame. It was to be the most incredible experience as we were to watch Bret 'The Hitman' Hart be inducted. After years of solitude, a stroke, distance from the WWE due to hatred for its owner and the loss of his own brother through a wrestling injury, it was understandable Bret's induction would perhaps come with some tension. His presence was sure to entice the fans of all fans to the Rosewood Theatre in Chicago Illinois. I paid over the odds for the seats but it was worth it. To see the most profiled wrestlers from days gone by and that of the current roster in addition to the late Eddie Guerreros family (a wrestler who had recently lost his life) was touching. I chose to wear a dress and Mark wore his kilt. Writing about this now, I still get emotional. He was so handsome. So smart. So patriotic. We hoped for an introduction or at least a view of Rowdy Roddy Piper.

We entered that theatre with excitement in our hearts and emotion in our souls. We knew there would be tears. We knew there would be laughter. Overall, we knew there would become memories. It was one of the best nights of my life. Cameras were not permitted due to media coverage but I can assure anyone that full night is embedded in my soul for days and years to come.

Bret Hart is and was the best wrestler to have lived. In my humble opinion of course. When he accepted his induction and appeared on stage, the crowd stood tall. The whole crowd. The front row. The back row, the waiting staff, the paparazzi, the families of the wrestlers; everyone. For his parting words:

"I want you all to know I am happy, I am healthy and I thank you all for coming out here

tonight"

That ended both Mark and I. We were so touched by his strength. I think it was at that point that I knew that no matter what pain a person feels, there is a point where you can turn a corner. It just so happens I took my subtle guidance from my favorite wrestler "The Hitman". God bless him and his pink glasses. Lord be thankful for the memories we made on that night.

But that was not to be the end of it. Far from it. Just the beginning.

We were shacked up in a Hilton Garden Inn. Was actually very nice. Included breakfast. Which was not cheap. We took in some city sights, food and opportunities to get out because Sunday night was to be THE night of all nights.

Chicago's All State Arena was to be home to WrestleMania 22. In addition, we had tickets. We also had huge jerseys from merchandise counter, of course setting us back money we didn't have BUT we still sported them and attempted to buy one of those really ridiculous foam fingers but they'd ran out. Thank god. Because they were stupid and unnecessary.

Now we were some hours behind in Chicago. I think around six so the wrestling at home was being televised at 2am. Mark was talking to his friend on text message who was trying to look out for us on TV. He could not see us obviously. What he could see though was someone in the 2nd row sporting a Celtic top. A bloody Celtic united top. I mean what are the actual chances of that? We rock up to a sports event in the United States and there is a Scot in the midst. It was hilarious.

A night of epic fighting took place. Best of which was pre-ceded by the entrance of the almighty Undertaker. If you are a wrestling fan, you will know what I am referring to. The chill that brings to a person when watching at home is something; can you imagine what it was like in person? AMAZING. Best moment ever.

The following day was the icing on an already deliciously calorific cake. Meeting my hero Shawn Michaels. The Heartbreak Kid. Standing in line at Borders book and music for 4 hours whilst they belted out James Blunts "Back to Bedlam" album was a challenge but then the sight of him set me alive. Jesus. I was screaming so loud Mark had to muzzle me with his hand. We were practically having a domestic except he was just as excited as I was and was trying not to lose his shit all together.

So we got to first in the queue. We were up next. Oh my word. All my days we insignificant in comparison to the moment I fell right at that hand shake. He hugged me. He actually hugged me. "HBK", Shawn Michaels, embraced this little Scottish lasso with the biggest heart and smile. He was warm, friendly, and so endearing to be around. He chatted to us about where we had come from, if we were enjoying the weekend and a staff member attempted a picture on our disposable camera. It was to be a mystery until developing if that picture or pictures would actually be decent. I really hoped they would be. They were not.

However, Monday night Raw followed and rounded off our weekend beautifully. The Monday night 'Raw' agenda after WrestleMania weekend usually sees some new talent come through and we were not disappointed.

It was a bloody epic night. I was sporting my new UGGS of course. Loving wearing warm clothes, being cozy in Chicago and watching my favorite pastime. It just resonated how happy I really felt at that moment. So content with life and easily pleased.

That was to be the last of our time as travelling lovers. I have the fondest of memories of that trip and would have loved to go to all WrestleMania's but as they are staged all over the USA it Is hard making a holiday out of some of the random places they chose so I tucked my dream of being a WM chaser safely in my pocket of pipe dreams. I guess you could say *we* called it a day.

In our relationship a mere few months later too.

Saddest time of my life.

11

Finding motherland

Having found love in a hopeless place in 2004 and having it end when my mind, body and soul was not prepared was toxic. More my own version of toxicity than the realistic scale it actually was. A relationship was over. I had not been the healthiest of people to be around in the last 6 months of our relationship as I had become somewhat derailed from normality. Often spending too much time thinking about money, holidays, materialism and self-critique that a mixture so evident to the human eye could cause nothing but distance was unbeknown to me and it was no surprise we drifted apart.

The reality of losing control of what I had become was so poignant because I was more of a mother figure losing my baby. He was my baby. I fed watered and looked after him, our home and had a never ending need and desire to control every element of his life to the point I had no doubt he had become detached from us and seen me more as "her". He loved me that I had no doubt but a long-term vision perhaps once evident and living happily in his plans, goals and ambition had taken the last train out of town. I suspect it was purely my desperation to keep control that kept him around for so long. That and the fact it was really his flat. Although we both owned it, it was always going to be his home. He had been there so long before I arrived I immediately felt like a stranger again. In the wrong way. Like all the time and effort I had injected into building a home for us was in jeopardy and I wondered how to keep my shit together without completely breaking down and begging him like the inner child I actually was. Not wanting to be abandoned. Again. An overwhelming sense of angst, misery and sadness swept over me that very day he left. I have always admired anyone who can go against the grain of what society teaches us to filter naturally; telling someone honestly you do not love them anymore or certainly not in the way you used to, cannot be easy. To offer zero filter to physical and emotional pain that is certain to take place when love is involved without actually wanting to cause said pain is a gift to deliver. Nevertheless, he remained dignified and I will always respect how hard that was for him for I loved and honored our commitment at that very moment. He gave the happiest time of his 20's to me. He was committed and supportive and for my very first relationship did all the right things to make me feel loved. It was an absolute miracle I rarely questioned his moves, his intentions and his plans. I just believed. To believe someone has true intent and your best interests at heart is a beautiful feeling. It secures your self-doubt in a locked casket. It brings such joy into your soul and warmth into your heart that you keep it tucked safely in your pocket so it is always near you. He was my best friend. In many ways, he was my only friend. He understood me. He tucked me in at night for I went to bed at like 8pm like a child on a routine. It is any wonder he seen me as the sexy lover I shoulda woulda coulda been. I laugh about that now.

The weeks to follow were a true misery. There is only so much friends and family can say or do in a time of sorrow that you appreciate or indeed listen to. You know they love you unconditionally and you know they want to take your pain away, but there is often a fine line between someone dictating advice to make you feel better AND just listening. No advice, no opinion, no "I told you so" just listening. Sometimes that is all you need is someone to virtually and physically hold your fragility in his or her hands as if it was a newborn.

If you think back to a time where someone offers their ear to listen or their hand to hold do you ever find yourself differentiating between the eager listener and the willing participant to your rehabilitation OR the cliché boasting societal conformist. There is a fine line.

Having a loving family is one thing and having some great friends and colleagues at a time where you feel the most alone is by no means a wonderful thing to have supporting your meltdown, but, to feel a huge void in the dark hole that is your inner feelings and loneliness is a hard hole to fill. Especially with the self-affirmations, it so richly needs at your most vulnerable time.

Morag was at the forefront of the "help Mel" campaign. She was and remains chairperson of the "help Mel get her shit together" society. It meets regularly you understand. For my life is a journey of torment and tantrums mixed with a shoe fetish and fierce neurosis.

It is any wonder she has not had her own meltdown at this point. I sucked the positivity out of her I am certain of it. I was on such a downer most days, going through the motions of adjusting to single life, bills bills bills and a huge worry I had personally been the catalyst to ruining the best thing that had ever happened to my life. But why? Why was I so down on myself? Was I accustomed to always thinking the worse of a situation that it was natural to me and in my mind to just introvert into my own subconscious? Yes. That is precisely what I did.

I had an idea. I decided to write a letter.

Now this is the age where pens and paper are still cool. Remember those days? Before

IPhone and Facebook poking being all the rage. When a person actually communicated by means other than a hashtag. Or a post about what you are having for dinner. Like the good old fashion days of olden times when you wrote a "dear john" and spilled your guts signed off with 'yours sincerely". I was always sincere in my articulation that was a certainty. So I started to write my letter. To whom you may ask? Well that is a very good question. To who. Who was the object of my literal affection? Affection; bit of a strange choice of word. Not sure if it was affection or if it was driven by desperation. A desperate attempt for attention or affection. The letter was addressed to Shirley. My mother.

The letter was written from my heart. With no bitterness, resentment or anger. It was a child asking her mother to love her. A child asking her own mother to show her love. Is that not something natural to a mother? I often wondered if fate or karma was repaying me (us) for actions in a previous life or whether being a child whose mother was not part of her childhood was just one of those things that happen to some people. Why did it happen to me? To my sister and I to my dad, to our family and to her. What happened to her that she felt the only escape was to leave her old life behind her and seek redemption elsewhere? Whilst the foundations of my letter were to ask for her love, I had also subconsciously created a list of questions to present to her for a suitable answer that only she could provide and there was a minimum pass mark of which I was not all that certain she would be able to meet. I knew nothing about her personality. Only tales told over the years gone by. Usually stemming from a family gathering where unnecessary conversations took place that caused pain to resurface without consideration for the lasting effects of a discussion no one really needed to have.

Now I undoubtedly had a wonderful caring family unit but I craved something from her that no one else was capable of providing me or fulfilling me with at that very moment. To seek comfort *a* mothers' arms was all my mind could think about.

I posted the letter. It was February 2007.

We were having a cold winter. I was frantic with worry about the ramifications of losing a household income (Mark) and having to go it alone on a measly salary so it was fair to say I was not in the most positive of mindsets. Misery guts right here! (Insert fist pump emoji).

And so the day came. Shirley called me. She did not write, she did not text message (although I am not certain she knew how! LOL), she did not email or send a carrier pigeon; she called. And I answered. On a rainy day outside HSBC where I had just finished my shift and was about to head home. Nope. Not before my heart stopped through shock as I was about to have my first adult conversation with my biological mother. Ironically, about whether she was prepared for the onslaught of my mental breakdown and need for her to wrap me up like sushi and snuggle me into a state of revitalized bliss. What an expectation. Well I feel that was only fair since she had given me fuck all to date. Like maybe a fiver now and then on a birthday or Christmas which bought me bus fares in and out of the town and a McDonalds big mac meal extra-large with strawberry milkshake; but that hardly a mother makes. True story right. Right?

Anyway, she called. So automatically, I was grateful. I let it ring too many times to be fair. I knew it was her. No one else I knew used a house phone and it was a Stirling number. Who actually uses a house phone anymore? Who needs 1000000 minutes to call other local numbers? Jesus. NO ONE MAN!

I answered. Breathless, voice shakes, that feeling in your gut of nerves. Remember the time you took your first driving test or the time, your first date went in for the kill and the nerves in the pits of your stomach just engulf your soul. My hands were shaking, palms were sweaty. Answer the phone Melanie. She is hardly going to bite you is she. She does not even know what you look like you absolute div.

"Hi Melanie, it's your mum"

BOOM. And a shocked expression surfaces on my cheeky chops. If only it was being filmed for candid camera I am certain my expression was classic.

Immediately I revert into child mode. Sad as that is I immediately yearned her help. Within 5 seconds, I am balling my eyes out telling her my woes. Boyfriend has gone, bills piling up, I am fat, I have no money and I am certain I have my heating on too high but I am fucked if I know how to turn it down. So there I am selling myself as the pinnacle daughter returning from the abyss, and she is no doubt at the end of the phone thinking who the hell is this retard. Not mine, she is not mine! Oh the irony. I am yours binto, you just forgot to come back after a dawnder to the shops!

She was actually very nice. Very warm and engaging. You would never have thought that it was our first proper conversation ever. We are not counting the drunken attempt at interaction that took place years previous.

So we are having this engaging conversation about my letter. She is speaking in a soft and polite way and I can tell she is just as nervous as I am. To the point, I feel for her. And it is I that needs the help. Perhaps she did too…

At this point, I have completely forgotten what utter shit I have spilled about in my letter. Forgetting that I have also attached a photo. Like she is my long lost pen pal. I mean honestly, what possessed me. She had to be reminded of my age? Of my gender? Of the fact she had a child? I find this humorous but all so true at the same time. So she starts reading my letter aloud to me. CRINGE. No Shirley this is not Jerry Springer and I do not need to be reminded of the pathetic whiner I am. I am all too aware at this stage.

This is textbook pushing someone away syndrome. Agreed?

I am so fixated on shielding myself from any more pain that my own intentions are now being fought by my desire to approach this conversation with speculation and skepticism. What is her game hmmmmm? Emmm, you wrote to her dafty. Let the woman speak.

I stop her mid-sentence. "Please help me. I am losing my identity. I feel lost, alone and not really sure what direction my life is taking now that I am adjusting to single life having been in my only ever loving relationship for the last 2.5 years".

"I will help you Melanie", she announces confidently. "Or I will at least try. Thank you for writing to me, I was pleased to receive your letter, although I am sad to hear of the events that have led to your letter."

She went into mother mode. It seemed to come to her naturally. Who knew!
All the while, I am still sitting in the car park of my work and colleagues and friends alike are now collecting their cars and suspiciously peering in my car window wondering who Mel is talking to and why she is balling her eyes out. And they all tap the window nervously to check I am not having an actual breakdown and I just courteously shoo them away signaling I am ok. Which exteriorly I am not however something internally triggers a feeling of comfort. For the first time I am engaging in a mother daughter discussion about life. With my mother, who is a stranger to my whole life and me? It was bizarre and fulfilling wrapped up a ball of Mary sunshine.

Shirley asks me rather tentatively if I would like to go and visit her. Without hesitation, I say yes. At this point, I do long for her embrace. Has she missed me? Has she missed us? Has she thought longingly and with hope that this day would come, albeit not necessarily under the circumstances where I am a crying mess of a wreck in need of a shake and double vodka.

She then escalated it to dinner. "Do you like Steak Pie", she says.

Fuck yes. Feed me that tasty goodness immediately. She is definitely in mother mode, I am still sitting in the car park bursting for a pee at this point, and I am certain rumors are rife that Mel is having a breakdown in her silver corsa.

Speaking of the Silver corsa. That is a story and a half.

So you remember Mark and I bought a Toyota MR2 Roadster. Beaut of a wee car so it was. Well when he upped and buggered off, I needed to think rationally about my expenditure and whilst at this stage I am still in a state of dismay, I did manage to resolve the car situation as soon as he left. That MR2 was a blood sucking money-draining pain in my ass. No matter how lovely it was to look at it, it was a bloody nuisance. For insurance, for fuel, for parts and for damage repair when some local pikey jumped on the roof and took a bottle of buckfast to the crease in the bonnet. Ruining it. Absolute dip shit.

Anyway, I know it is worth a good few thousand so I decide to trade it in for a brand new car or a car that is only 1-year-old. Smart huh? I had found a remaining brain cell and used it to negotiate a deal for a 2006 silver corsa, demo, never sold, still possessing the fresh car smell and off I trotted into the sunset with this magnificent car that costs a fraction in insurance, fuel and my sanity. No convertible though. Sad times. Well considering Scotland had not seen summer since Jesus was a boy; it was hardly a great loss now was it? Laughs aloud.

So I am sitting there, arse is numb by this point but I am dreaming of Steak Pie and I am numb to the fact that I am engaged in a conversation with a human being who just happen to give birth to me. And I like it. Whether I like the idea of the steak pie or her embrace in my life, I am not sure what takes precedence since it is dinnertime and I am starved. Well I say starved but looking at my body, I am not actually starved.

And so, the call begins to wrap up. Like a Christmas present destined for a happy recipient. A date is set. I am going to visit her. I am actually going to see my Mum.

A few days separated that call and the actual date of visiting her.

In that time, I knew in my heart of hearts I had to go and speak to my dad. And my step mums, explain my intention and my rationale, and hope that they understood. Whilst I did not need or look for their permission, I did not want to be left feeling as if I had betrayed them. I wanted to be honest.

I went to my parents the following night. My dad sat silent and my step mum, Morag sat listening intently.

They both acknowledged my plight. They could see the pain in my eyes and if this was to be an avenue of redemption for me then they were not going to stand in my way. They advised that they understood. I knew there was for sure an element of hurt on their part. I had inflicted unintentional hurt on them. Their choice to mask that in favor of preserving my self-respect was noble. My dad, not one to say much or give much away was cautiously calm. Looking at me with glazed eyes. I did not question him. I dare not poke emotion out of him at such a vulnerable time for a conversation so I just accepted their "approval" to proceed and said my goodbyes. I needed this for me. For however long the need for her would last, I did not know, but even if it was to be a temporary euphoria in my life; it was still going to happen and I needed to live with no regrets and instead take a chance. Of all the chances to take, this was up there with the most important for my journey at that moment in time.

A sleepless night ensued as I prepared for my dinner date with the devil.
What do you wear to dinner with "the parent" I asked myself? As if it was meeting the boyfriends mum for the first time except it was my mum. HAHA. Do I appear overly keen and dress for Sunday best? On the other hand, do I keep it casual and let her see I am a strong confidant woman, only mildly falling to pieces on the inside? It was a tough call but I opted for warmth no matter what fashion crisis I presented to the masses. It is February remember and stiff nipples and a long wait for inner car warmth are all the rage. It is absolutely Baltic outside. So much so, Toby never wanted to go outside for the majority of autumn/winter. He looked at me with daily disgust at the thought of me suggesting he take himself outside for a wander each day. "Aye ok mum, I will go out here AWWWW day whilst you are at work and freeze my paws off waiting on your return". Jog on my friend was the only way I could summarize his facial expression.

7pm dinner was imminent. Now what was the appropriate etiquette? Do I just go straight into eating? Alternatively, do I ask questions? It was confusing state. Do I cuddle her or shake her hand? Do I wait for her to ask me to sit down or just take a seat? She will no doubt ask if I want a drink; do I say vodka or tea. I mean the questions in my mind were endless. For fuck sake Melanie calm doon. It is no wonder I found myself single. I was irritating as shit. I irritated myself.

The drive was to take me 20 minutes. In those 20 minutes, I listened to James Morrison. Because in 2007 he was popular. Mixed with a little Paolo Nutini, it was a nostalgic and quant car journey. I had mixed excitement, sickness, nerves and humility for what was about to happen. A text message from my friend Kelly (more on her later but she too was going through her own break up), and I was setting upon Shirley's street corner with ease. Parked. Hand break on and breathe.

She was already at the door. Fuck. Get out the car. Get out the car. Get out the car. It felt like days before I dragged my arse out of the car and locked the door. Make eye contact.

I looked up. Our eyes met. She said hello. I said hello. I walked up her path towards her front door that had two or three steps to get into the house. I stopped at the steps waiting for her to invite me in. I did not really know how to be. Isn't that strange? It felt strange. I was not sure if her husband would also be there. Turns out, he was not.

"Would you like to come in?" she said.

I slowly etched up the stairs and it felt natural and fitting to embrace her. When she hugged me, I broke down in tears. As if all my days gone by had led to this moment, where I could release my torn demons onto her shoulders and let the tears and misery escape my tortured self.

She hugged me until my tears stopped. She did not seem awkward and instead it seemed to fit her naturally and her ability to comfort me in that moment was truly blissful. Albeit part of me was slightly reserved in kissing her. The hug was more than enough. It lasted longer than a normal hug but not too long that it was weird. It completely broke any awkward silence and solidified the need for this event to take place and be everything it needed to be.

I sat down on her sofa. She sat opposite me. We stared each other down for a little while. Not in a gang initiation type way or anything; just in an "I am not sure how or what to be right now but I am ok with being here with you in your home" type of manner. Her house was cozy. Like super warm and very homey. Not as warm as the furnace of my flat considering I could not work my heater and it was 904 degrees all the livelong day but warm nonetheless was her abode.

I immediately jumped into absolute bullshit small talk. It was like a survival guide to being a dick. Just keep talking Melanie she will not notice that you are a blabbering mess. Oh, yes she will. She has. She puts her hand up and asks, "Are you ok, would you like a drink". "Vodka, got any vodka?" "No, you are driving, I will make you tea". "Aye ok". Chastised within my first 5 minutes for being a total pikey. I appreciated her sentiment right enough. Those roads were scary on a winter's night so I could not really fault her. Moreover, she might not have been a vodka drinker you know. I just presumed everyone loved the Smirnoff.

So I start sipping my tea and he voice is so smooth. Like a sweet lullaby, she feeds my ego. Telling me how much of a mature young lady I am, how strong I must be and how she is impressed with my strength. And I am sitting there thinking to myself wow, she actually likes me. Yet I have not said much of essence or relevance. However, she does know I am heartbroken.

She appeals to my inner child. This is of course the whole reason I wrote to her in the first place.

She comes over, sits next to me, and hugs me as I can feel my eyes fill with tears once again. She says it is all going to be ok and she places both hands simultaneously around my arms to keep me embraced until I feel her warmth.

She gives herself to me selflessly. No agenda. She listens to my tears and does not ask too many questions. She just sits there letting me get it all out. Like I have been bottling up a sorrow for years and now is the moment, it felt right to break the seal.

Then boom, out of nowhere a tall lean strapping young lad appears from upstairs…

Hi, I am James. Your brother. Oh brother where art thou.

Now had this moment been captured by Cilla Black for Surprise Surprise I was definitely meeting the criteria for "look shocked, emotional and a little scared at the same time".

The evening turned into a comforting and rather pleasant night. I exchanged banter with James (and Shirley) for hours. It was as if it just fitted. Surreal but nostalgic to think back now on the happiness I felt but whilst it was a happy notion; the tortured torment that lay beneath was only going to surface more and more as I removed the barriers to my heartstrings.

2007 springtime arrived and the dynamics of my family unit changed significantly. I cannot explain the innate desire I had to be in her company any more than a daughters' desire to be in her mothers' company as pure natural need for a mothers' touch. Even though I had immense guilt writhing in me, every day for the pain I must have placed on my dad and Morag was constantly on my mind. Classic anxiety 101.

Shirley possessed a certain "je ne sais pas" about her. She was reserved but clearly friendly and delighted to have me in her life. Visiting her, going shopping together, learning about each other. I use the term "learning" loosely because learning would require complete commitment to the cause. I immediately accepted that Shirley came with a deep filter. A filter she was not prepared to dust off even if it meant I begged.

I promised myself that whilst I wanted to talk openly and freely about the impact she has had on my life both positively and negatively (and contrary to expectation it has seen some good moments), I do not have a desire to disrespect her in an offensive manner purely for momentum.

I did not love her. I did not know her. I wanted to know her. I wanted her to know me. I wanted her to want to know me. To know of my childhood and my fears. To know how it felt waking up on Christmas mornings without my mum hugging me and telling me Santa had been. To know how it felt graduating primary school singing the class anthem and not having my mum standing watching and cheering me on. I wanted her to feel my pain. I did not realize all along that she harbored her own pain. Her own "counsel" as she put it. That alone must have burdened her shoulders as it showed on her expression anytime an awkward subject arose or was presented for discussion.
Sure Ed Sheeran could write a song about the world of words that should have come out then…

Probing her in a subtle manner had to become second nature to me. For my natural desire to know "stuff" would not go away. And she handled that impressively. Trying where possible to offset her lack of want to fuel my curiosity by feeding me glorious meals. Like who doesn't love a steak pie dinner. And pudding. Actual pudding. No wonder I had fat mess written all over me.

Then came the outstanding invite to the bright lights of New York City. A holiday paid for she said. All I needed was my spending money she said. Sign me up I SAID! Wow. Whilst my life long desire and eagerness to grace the big apple with my miserable mentality had been itching to come to fruition I would be lying if I said I wasn't just as happy that I would get time alone, with my mother, away from life. I envisaged 25 years' worth of love, kisses, hugs, walks, pats on the back, discussions about boys, discussions about friends, talks of fashion, health, ambition, career, education, family and us. The happiness

of thinking about that notion burst my heart wide open. The countdown to November 2008

was a long one.

Long ass countdown to the best trip of my life. I saved. I saved hard.

The months ahead did leave me feeling elated. Like a weight had shifted from my

shoulders. However, I did continue to harbor guilt and resentment of myself for feeling as

if I had betrayed my dad and Morag. Never once did they contribute to that feeling intently

but I did have to think before I spoke in terms of my plans, movements etc. as occasionally

my dad would ask what I was up to and if I had plans to be with Shirley then I found it

awkward to discuss. Therefore, it was always easier to lie. I had the best of intentions to

preserve his feelings always. I perhaps just did not show it too well.

I always felt bad about that. Guilty sad. The sad you define in your conscience as dis-

pleasing to someone you seek approval from. This is of course how my inner child will

always behave when it comes to the approval of my dad. My hero. My guardian and my

savior.

I think back to those months and remember distinctively the poker face mentality my

parents had to perfect. I am genuinely sorry for that pain but ironically, they will argue

they were happy for me. I guess my perception of their feelings is just that. A perception. I

am not them and could not possibly surmise their exact conversations or thoughts unless

they actually told me. One thing I do know is Morag adopting a more specific protective

tone in her approach to keeping me safe from any emotional hurt. Whilst she herself must

have felt unappreciated or unwanted in terms of me looking elsewhere for a mother, I most

definitely felt she was ready for battle should I break down and cry with sheer

disappointment at a moment's notice. Like her blood was simmering like a toxic volcano

and a ticking time bomb waiting for Shirley to fuck up and ruin my life. On the other hand, perhaps not as dramatic as that but you get my point eh? I do not think I have ever loved Morag as much as I did at that moment in time. Could it be that what I was searching for in Shirley was already more than present in my Morag? My mum. My angel. The desire to protect your child I am certain must be innate to the point it is a knee-jerk reaction to life. I feel that her desire was so powerfully fueled during those months the more I became excited to go on a trip with essentially someone who could completely destroy my restored faith in humanity. Whilst I was far from healed in terms of feeling low about the various things that occupied by torn mind; I was feeling adrenalin daily at the prospect of travelling with a companion who paid no rent but occupied space in my heart.

Then came question time from Ashleigh. This actually surprised me. I honestly suspected that no matter how involved I became with Shirley, she would never back down from her hatred of the past even though I know now she chooses to adopt a forgive and forget approach as it gives her clearer mindset. Although in 2007 and 2008 it was a different side to her, I witnessed. What was usually a "martyr" approach to life; never giving anything personal away; keeping everything to herself; not sharing with me (which was ok as we weren't compelled to be friends); not really chatting socially BUT still retaining respect and love for each other as siblings…she showed real depths of vulnerability when she asked if she could also come to Shirley's with me. I asked her why. What did she want out of it as I did not want to share Shirley in a complacent way? By nature, Ashleigh and I are so very different. She is laidback, cool calm and collected whereas I am more of a control freak looking for clarity in everything. Everything. I had no desire to confuse Shirley or myself by contributing to Ashleigh's objective or motive. She needed to do that herself. This was not the time or place in our maturing adulthood to be pining for the love and affection of our mother together. It was to be a singular path of individuality. Because Shirley owed us that at least and we owed it to ourselves.

The humility and want for an emotional reunion though, in Ashleigh's eyes, was something I grew to admire more in my sister. Whilst I always looked up to her in terms of age and life experience, I felt like she needed me to be the support when that initial reunion took place. I will never forget her eyes, her body language, he fears, her desire for it to be a memorable experience.

Forgiveness was a strength I did not possess at that moment in time. And neither did she. Even in the midst of my euphoric confusion, I did keep in mind that only when I could tell my story without crying or feeling pain, would I consider myself healed from the past.

That took courage. Nevertheless, it also took time. And it was not time that stood in our way to a path of least resistance; it was her. We collectively needed to feel her penance.

I very quickly established a feeling of subtle jealousy that Ashleigh was involved at all. For I had mentally prepared for Shirley to be something "for me". And me only. As if I had always felt sharing my dad was too much. As sad as that is, her physical being meant I had something. Something that was mine. An endless source of fuel for my contentment to breed on.

I felt suggesting myself and Ashleigh see her at different times. Ironically like making appointments to see your shrink. Of which she was highly under-qualified that I am certain of. In fact, I would put money on the fact she would not know how to speak about her own shoes without having her own "counsel" on why they were dirty. So open mindedness was not to be her strong point and thus a collective 3-way gathering was not on my agenda, no matter how complacent Ash felt about any arrangement. I wanted my own time, my own night and to feel like the attention I craved was directed at me only. After years of living, without I felt I deserved that at least.

No amount of birthday cards with a fiver in them once a year was ever going to be suitably replaced by a family gathering. I needed to feel more presence from Shirley. I needed to feel her love. Her commitment to me as a person, as a daughter, as *her* daughter. It was like pulling teeth. Always so compliant, cooking for me, texting, offering to do stuff…but did she listen? Did she offer to talk about the questions on the cusp of my tongue every single minute of every single day? No, that was not on the table. I accepted she was waiting to see how important that was to me. To us. I found this to be the most hurtful act of all. She felt she needed to wait instead of taking immediate action to rectify a very evident pain in each of us.

Therefore, what would become routine etiquette would eventually become the enemy.

Therefore, I took my jolly self to hers for regular dinners and played the dutiful daughter. I would be lying if I said that did not give me some delight absolutely. I did not really engage with Ashleigh in terms of cross reference analysis on what each of us got out of it, partly because she told me nothing! LOL. Essentially, though the process of building a relationship with my own mother came with benefits. She bought me unnecessary shit but I saw that as her way of paying her dues. Could have been doing with new shoes in primary five doll but hey whatevs!

New York was just around the corner before I knew it. My arse at this stage was about the same size as the Big Apple. I had gained so much weight I was a walking jelly baby. Nevertheless, New York still beckoned and I was beside myself with anticipation and excitement to see everything that I had ever seen on TV. The *good life* I liked to refer to it as. It was as if my subconscious wanted to be completely lost in a vortex of pulp fiction. A world of bright lights and pretty colors. A world where the earth is enough love to keep you grounded but where you would have to pay millions of dollars to live in a shed. Denial was rife but I did not care.

Shirley was equally excited. I anticipated her nerves about the only alone time she would essentially have no escape from, with me, since she went for bread when I was 2 and never returned. I would be lying if that did not give me some sick gratification that she would find that slightly uncomfortable. Feed my ego oh dear mother ship.

12

What is the story mother glory?

Writing this many years later, and as you would expect having taken some time I am now older in years, albeit not many, than when I originally started; my emotions and perspective have changed. Some for the better and some for the worse.

I would like touch on this briefly to give some insight into my mind in 2010 when my relationship with Shirley had peaked. At only 3 years. Like a soulless marriage of hearts that had beaten their last breath.

Having harbored resentment, sorrow, desire for more, desperation and willingness to have a normal family structure since I was very little; the fact my efforts, in my eyes, during the time I was reunited with my mother weren't nourished in a way my expectations had imagined; paved the way for the end of an era.

Having only felt real love and affection in terms of biological affection from my dad for the former early years (and until Morag came along), my innate sense of belonging had been cruelly crushed at the most pivotal stage of cognitive learning. I believe wholeheartedly that the anticipation of failure, relationship breakdown capacity and that of trust in later life was something the sceptic in me anticipated from the age of three. It is in no way a reflection of love I received from my home. My childhood home will always fill my cheeks with a smile drawn from my most cherished box of memories.

The emotional force to understand something at a young age is tough. Obviously, at 3 years old, I was not in a position to sit and analyze my parents' marriage issues and my mother's subsequent exit from the Crystal maze; but I did possess an emotional attachment to my mother that could not just remove itself from my soul. Why would that ever be expected of any child? I certainly do not think It was expected of me or Ashleigh but I think the conscious efforts to protect and serve our best interests as children, from a capacity of loving home, schooling, routine and health were the catalyst for the "life goes on" approach I know quickly developed. With my dad relying heavily on support from Shirley's family as well as his own. And rightly so.

In my later years, I was to learn just how tough that time was for him. As a man and as a father to two small children, in the 80's, at the height of the economic depression. A young man, in his early twenties abandoned. Whether at fault in his marriage or not, he was still abandoned with very little financial stability; two small children who do not even know what is happening and the end of a marriage he may or may not have seen coming.

Iain Hume, my dad. A beautiful creature. A rare breed of human kindness that I am so very blessed to have in my life. Always supportive, albeit his chat frequency is pish now I am in my 30s and he is off swanning the comedy circuit. More on that later...

A beautiful soul indeed. Painful to discuss something so personal absolutely but the curiosity always presided in me. What happened? Why did she go? Why did she not take us with her? Because he would not let her.

My dad, my hero, refused to allow more disrupt to our lives, put his own heartbreak to the back of his mind, and put our heartbreak to the forefront of his utmost priorities. That takes a soldier full of courage and bravery to overcome that type of grief, I can only imagine.

I have only ever had one conversation with my dad regarding this. It always evokes such raw emotion in me even considering approaching the subject as I have a lifelong need to protect him in any shape I think will succeed. As a family, we were out one night. I recall we went to the SECC to see Peter Kay in 2011 and upon return to the family home, the four of us, my dad, me, Ash and Morag sat down. Conversation was never focused on the past, far from it but the type of conversation that was to take place that evening was to be pivotal in the restoration of faith. Unscripted and unplanned it was perhaps act of fate that led our conversation to an argument between myself and Ashleigh that required mediation from my dad, leading to tears a plenty and an emotional heart-to-heart between he and I. Long overdue I may add. It has not happened since. However, once in a lifetime is surely better than nothing at all.

Sat next to my dad in my childhood home hugging his shoulder, remembering the days of younger years when his shoulder was the safest sanctuary I had. It was the only sanctuary I had. Revisiting that reinforcement of parent/child affection was a beautiful thing. What started as my dad trying to keep peace and harmony led him to elaborate briefly on the reasons he was so keen to just keep a tranquil home, mind and outlook on life. At that moment having felt immense pressure on my own guilt for betraying him (albeit that is not what he ever made me feel); I was essentially looking for a story of reassurance to retain my self-respect that he still loved me regardless. Regardless of running back to something that destroyed us.

He told me a story. The hardest story a daughter can hear from her father.

"Melanie, you're my lassie. You and Ashleigh. I love you both with all my heart. I fought to keep you. Not once, in my life did I consider giving you away which would have undoubtedly been the norm in the eighties but I refused to let anyone take anything from you or me. Your mother decided to leave. She was not happy. It destroyed me but most of all I wanted to protect you and your sister from the hurt of knowing the why's and where's. You would only feel confusion and at that time I had enough confusion for all of us"

Now looking into the eyes of my dad at that particular point, I saw his pain. I saw years of raw pain glistening in his eyes ready to escape with what looked like a lifetime of relief from letting go of the hurt. He had tears in his eyes. The eye contact was a realization that I was not his little girl anymore. I had a lifetime of abandonment in me that needed to feel some justification through only his words.

He went on to tell me the story of how he had to take us both to Stirling Miners Welfare for a scheduled meeting on the mining fiasco and as club secretary his presence was necessary. Not showing any real emotion it was of course going to be a subject of curiosity as to why Iain was there with his two girls. He did not have anyone else. He would not allow anyone else to take us.

I listened hard that night. Still listening he went on to show physical emotion. His eyes filled with tears and depths of his torture became all too clear. My dad, a young man at the time had his life completely destroyed; had two small kids to contend with; a mind full of confusion and worry and a serious employment issue effecting Scotland and the economy. The absolute fear of not been able to provide for your children must have been horrific.

I am bawling my eyes out at this point in the night. Like truly, mascara is down my face on my nips ken!

He is actually consoling me at this point and yet he is the one with the life story worthy of empathy. I listened hard. I kept eye contact and when I asked the question "why didn't you allow her to take us Dad", he responded because "you were my girls" and "you weren't going anywhere".

If that is not the definition of unconditional love, I really do not know what is.

In that moment, he smiled. The smile he always and has always given to comfort me. To make me feel like I belong. I have a supporter and advocate in my life and he is that. He was and is a superhero and I was now to question what my superpower in life was to be if I was to really do his efforts justice.

We talked for a long time. And those feelings of wondering if I would ever have such special and sacred moments again, returned with one eyewink. Yes, my dad had suffered but he had forgiven and moved on. And I had to learn to do the same. For my own sanity at the very least. I learned so very much that night. I learned that my dad did not have a resistance to talking; he just did not have words that truly represented his emotions and I respect and still respect that to this very day. I felt closer to him than ever on that night. Overcome with exhaustion our parting thoughts and unwritten understanding what that should I ever find not able to look on the bright side; I would find him sitting next to me in the dark. Always and not necessarily in person.

A mere 3 months earlier, I had written a letter. To Shirley. Yes, another one, because clearly I am a drama queen and like to revisit the olden times to get my point across.

Anyway, I decided after an inner turmoil of question over just what I was gaining out of our relationship, realistically and what had become so cumbersome and regimented that the value had diminished. I needed to take action. A permanent action.

Arguably looking back now 6 years later (I am finally in 2016!) yes it has taken me that long to write my stories...do not judge! ASSHOLE!

Looking back, I could have perhaps been less dramatic in my approach to walking away. I constructed my letter at work.

Once written I printed. Once printed I enveloped. Once enveloped I took it to my dad and Morag, my mum. My only real mum I ever needed. I ever truly needed. So going forward she is now labelled as mum. She will always occupy space in my heart as my mum, biological or not. The disjoint of not seeking her comfort or indeed feeling her comfort and back in 2007 when I reached out to Shirley Is something perhaps fate was left to teach me.

And so the letter. A letter written with depth, humility, raw authenticity, emotion, fear, hope and a pinch of faith was to create a message of closure. With a twist. With an opportunity for her to completely remove herself from her comfort zone of keeping her past under lock and key; but to at least, acknowledge that we, her children had to come out of OUR comfort zone to ask our own mother to love us. That is something you will not find many children having to admit to themselves.

It was written with love above all else. Love for her as my mother. Love for her as a human being who had gone through her own pain in life and love for her as a woman who dealt with the hand she was given in the only way she felt safe and knowing all those years ago. I put my empathy down to my core values and how my dad raised us. To smile. To forgive and to live. As that is the key to inner happiness ultimately.

I drafted a long note. Discussing things that etched on my mind more regularly than they should and it did not feel instinctively healthy for me to sustain a rather empty approach to being in her company. I explained there was no real significant time or place that my feelings changed but overall I felt that in the 3 years we had attempted to develop something real; there was something very apparent; her lack of communication. I tried to write in a reasonable way that did not enforce my expectations on her and deem her a failure because she did not live up to my expectations. I did however; explain clearly and rationally that I really just longed to establish a real bond after so many years apart. I felt sad writing that in a way that she would understand. Ironically, I did not harbor a feeling that she knew me at all. Hence, the letter was critical for my self-esteem.

Please talk to me Shirley. Please tell me what went on regardless of how much you think it will hurt me, hurt my sister or hurt my dad. Her consistent approach to filtering her words was the running theme of my plea letter. I touched on her family; her husband and her son, whom I had developed a really harmonious and affectionate relationship with. I praised them for giving her the happiness as a woman she deserved after what must have been a tough enough period of her past that warranted her walking away from her two children in the first place. I refused to accept it was all for nothing.

I thanked her extensively for the materialistic and non-materialistic experiences she afforded me in that 3-year period; of which New York City was one of them. I praised her handling of her only grandchild; Cora, Ashleigh's daughter albeit I did point out that I felt she was subconsciously tying to repay her "debts" to us by spoiling Cora to the point that it became obvious and wasn't going to teach Cora any values on respect and appreciation. I also felt that was a slap in the face to me. I felt the need to remind her I was her daughter, not a pen pal. Not an old school friend. I was her *daughter*. Why was it so hard for her to treat me like that? Did I even know how to accept love as a daughter? From my mother's perspective? Perhaps not. Perhaps that was the issue all along.

One of my questions to her whilst writing was "do you think I am damaged", "unfixable"? That was a hard enough topic to touch on. I was essentially asking my birth mother to admit that her actions ruined my chance at a normal cognitive development.

The anger in me whilst writing did elevate at times. I felt such disappointment that I had tried so hard to just mold into this mum/daughter jigsaw that the harder I could feel it becoming the lonelier I felt in myself. It was an incredibly lonely time. She was my friend. I felt like I had a new friend who surely valued me enough to save us.

My letter was a desperate attempt to force her to fight for me. Was I worth the effort? I was not entirely sure. Should a child ever feel that way? Absolutely not.

The letter was demonstrating my pain. Simple as that. At that moment in time having experienced all I thought I was going to ever experience in terms of her raw honesty and ability to tell me her version of events for all intense purposes just to give me understanding and closure; my only uninterrupted avenue of channeling my feelings to her was by writing it all down. Oh the irony…

And so the letter was finished. It was finished on 15 November 2010. I took it to my mum and dad to read it aloud. I needed to encompass my grief, my apology for inflicting any residual hurt on them, my desire to seek something from Shirley she had yet to part with and my overall weakened ability to understand my own thoughts amalgamated in this one sitting, reading aloud my letter asking my own mother to love me.

Tears were shared. They both knew how much it meant to me and how hard I had worked to try to gain momentum with her. Morag showed real sympathy to me. She was a mother. She felt completely helpless as clearly could not take that heartbreak away. My dad, sitting quietly (remember this is a few months before the heart-to heart), offers very little in the way of verbal support BUT looks disgusted that it has come to this. Like he knew all along she would not instill something in me I longed for, I needed. In essence and in later years, I would learn to realize that this had to come from within. Enough self-love always outranks reaching out from others.

My mum offered to send the letter recorded delivery that ensured it would be received and signed for. Now you could argue this was a bold and unnecessary move to get her to listen but I had reached my limits in terms of trying. I needed something. I was feeling so detached from my own understanding of the dynamics of our acquaintance this was more an S.O.S to her. A last ditch attempt to shake things up.

So it was sent. And I went on business the following day. Overnight in Birmingham. To return on the Thursday…the day it would be received by her. Surely I would get a call from her asking to speak, surely she would be disappointed I felt that way and surely her innate desire to protect her child (albeit something she learned in her latter years from our perspective) …surely she would listen. Not to respond immediately. But to listen.

Arriving home on that Thursday night to a text message from her son, my half-brother, was about as blunt a move I had ever been privy to. His choice of cruel words to highlight my ungratefulness (LOL!), my lack of understanding and my inability to appreciate everything *she had done for me* royally tipped my mental stability over the edge. I was stunned. For two reasons. Firstly, why was he privy to that letter so soon? Secondly, why had she not reached out to me? And why not chuck in a third? Who the fuck did he think he was with his macho attempt at chastising me in a derogatory way implying I was a traitor for simply asking her to love me. Note, his words implying comparison of 3 years of involvement to a lifetime of abandonment as some sort of penance, It was no surprise I felt he was demanding she now be completely removed from the emotional sentence.

I was stunned beyond comprehension. Distraught at the presence of conflict and hatred fueling my already existing emotional state of mind, I really did not know where to turn.

How to cope with the grief?

I can only relate the pain to losing a person through death. In an instant she had been someone I hoped to overcome her own demons and embrace the chance to really connect with me; instead, she became my enemy by proxy because of her sons' choice of spiteful and bitter words. What did he know exactly? Did he experience our childhood? Did he watch his own mother slowly disappear from his memory? Did he go through his entire childhood wondering why his mother did not want him? No, he did not.

He gained from our loss and whilst his macho, egotistical, immature approach at lashing out to defend his mums honor was to an extent somewhat understandable; he added fuel to an already existing fire and compounded the issue tenfold. It was so far beyond unnecessary it destroyed any hope I had that my dreaming could indeed come to fruition. Instead, it ignited hatred in my mind. If ever I was to adopt a "life is just too god damn short" mantra it was on that day, at that moment, for the very reason that I did not want to spend another day chasing a ghost. Deem a dream that should and would never a dream be had she actually shown any normal maternal behavioral traits.

A chapter was ending. The weeks that followed seen her halfhearted attempt at reconcile. A mediocre text message offering time at her house to chat was about as useful as a chocolate fireguard. The damage was done. Had I not experienced enough of a knock back? Had the rejection I was naively encouraging not enough to set me free? I really wish I possessed the carefree complacency she had mastered but I was sad. Sad it had all come to an abrupt end. However, walking away and living my own life my way without chasing the wind anymore was to be my biggest strength in life. Who is she to dictate the space occupied in my sorrow? No-one.

The rest was still unwritten but for now my most intense and unstructured relationship was to be a mere memory. Of which there were pleasantries but not enough to occupy any more space in my motto biographical tales of days gone by. Oh no sirree. I was sad to be walking away from the steak pie though. She could have at least taught me how to cook. Cow.

Life was to change. I needed a sharp taste of reality. A new person to occupy the role of "first person to tell good news to". I did like sharing with her. But no more.

Walking away from her also meant walking away from my extended family. I would later realize that it was easier than I had ever imagined. This clearly meant I was stronger than I ever gave myself credit for and had protected my heart just a little more than I had thought. This made me proud. But also a little nostalgic that I had clearly represented the notion of skepticism to its fullest extent. Perhaps I had anticipated her disappointing my expectations all along.

Expectations. Something this whole experience taught me to try and refrain from. Living with your own limits but setting your heart free of hatred or pain was to be my new mantra come 2011.

First…I was to meet a real dick of a guy. Who tortured my head up royally! He taught me a valuable lesson. In internet dating and meeting the narcissist of all narcissists. A completely new level of 'cray cray'. Internet dating…the new chapter…

13

Chapter change

Internet dating. Is that not *just* the most ludicrous thing that has ever shit all over our generation of wannabe egos searching for our souls' counterpart in another?

Selling yourself as a young 30 something who likes reading and listening to music. When in fact statistically we are all a little mentally unhinged with abandonment issues successfully swinging through life on our trapeze of cat loving, carb eating, Cosmo drinking insecurities. Searching for a love that compounds your every heartbeat because all the materialism in the world just doesn't cut it until you wake up next to someone who tickles your fancy providing they don't have dog breath in the morning. Moreover, preferably who IS sporting a sizeable penis so the world can be a better place and your vagina is a happy camper. Why is this shit so difficult to come by? For fuck sake.

Uploading pictures pre "filter years" was an easy task. Find the best, add to profile and publish. Plenty of Fish was all the rage in 2010. I decided to join at the latter end of the year, post Shirley gate. You know, feed my ego, meet a few 'hotties', and see what all the fuss was about. "Sign up now". Yes, please. Immediately regretting it but finding it incredibly difficult to resist lurking online like a grooming maniac searching for an eager but completely naïve victim to feed my ego. And maybe buy me dinner.

Now you have to remember in case you weren't already aware after nearly 50000 words of "woe me" chat LOL, I am a traditionalist and old romantic and whilst I have tried to modernize my own take and approach to this mantra in my life, the core values of my heart's desire is arguably what 99% of the nation want. They just do not know it or admit to it. I was neither. I oozed a slight desperation in my attempt to attract someone with the same mantra. When in fact time is all it was ever going to take…still waiting as a write this at age 34 now…beside the point goddamn it.

Being the articulate scholar that I am I felt my profile was bang on. Perhaps a bit condescending to the fuck boys of society and yet the cesspit of POF options still sent the "how's you" messages in their hundreds. Well my darling I am fine. Why is there a need I wonder to adopt an interview type introductory approach to a conversation? You'

Obviously fine. You are a strong confidant woman Melanie. But all the criteria you pretend you don't use as a pre-checklist to even replying "I am fine thanks" rapidly turns full circle when you see golden brown eyes and a six pack on some hot boys' fine choice at a profile picture. Even before filters allowed a change of race LOL. So hot boy 101 messages me this one night. I am like yes please. Car salesperson from Hamilton. Groomed and sexy I immediately think yes he has potential. What the fuck did I know man? Jesus. Denial. Honestly. Anyway, he feeds me the cheesiest lines known to humanity and clearly possesses less than the mentally retarded brain cells but he makes me laugh. Therefore, I agree to meet him for a date. Apparently, I have a nice smile. Aye pal many a year in braces gave me my Colgate inspired smile. Wait until you see the size of my ass though young car salesperson, 34 from weegie land. I will cool off on the whole self-pity now. Enough is enough. I was a sexy and sassy little number, albeit a little needy but hey who is perfect!

So the day of the date arrives. He rocks up with a hangover and less than the gorgeous idealistic future husband view I had in my mind but his banter was on point. We enjoyed a meal at Behind the Wall in Falkirk followed by 16 thousand cocktails and before we knew it we were pretending we were on our 10-year anniversary date night and convincing other patrons just that. What a pair of absolute Fannies. Of course, we then ended up back at mine, naked and happy. How all good nights out should end? Perhaps just not absolutely ringoed and with a stranger I understand. Let us refer to it as the experimental years. (Sorry mum!) …

What we failed to realize was that the countries sickest winter blizzards were to piss all our Monday morning parade the next day. So whilst we were sparkled preparing for the hangover of all hangovers, the streets of sunny Camelon was to become a winter wonderland. Making it a work from home day for me but an absolute nightmare for mongoose weegie (about to explain how he acquired this name just wait!) to get to work. No trains and no transport. Plus, he was starting a new job. Yet he was ejected from my home quick smart, as I actually did need to get to work. Never once did it cross my mind that I would hear from him again. But fuck me he was quick smart. Message after message affording me compliment after compliment. Now bear in mind I cannot add any materialistic value to this assholes life but me. Just me. Perhaps a little banter was all he wanted. He certainly needed a lot more help in a number of ways I can assure you of that. Big fat mistake replying to him.

Anyway, it turns out he was a master of emotional abuse. Manipulation stemming from either a hatred of his lack of extensive wealth or the complete opposite. Neither of which I could establish accuracy. I could not quite pinpoint what it was that niggled at my gut instincts. Do not get me wrong he was the doting boyfriend, buying me flowers, Adele's new album, taking me for dinner, providing me with affection and the like BUT the big fat elephant in the room was I just was not sure he was stable. He would make me feel like I walked on eggshells. Perhaps my own insecurity of him leaving me did contribute largely to me adopting a "pleasing" mantra and always running after him like some child. But I stand proud of the instincts I listened to. I knew something was up. He was careless with his money. I just could not trust his integrity for some reason. Typical salesman banter I put it down to initially. Then Christmas morning came and an all expenses trip to New York City was gifted to me. Helicopter tour, plaza suite and a limo transfer taboo, meanwhile my gift to him was a Hollister hoodie and a new mug. Girlfriend of the year I was clearly not. I am sitting there at his house on Christmas morning in my finest pants thinking to myself…right Melanie this is the nicest and best present ever BUT he has zero personal items in this flat and an old TV…he has a furnished rental and he is a compulsive liar about his property, wealth, cars and general life. What is he hiding? This was the beginning of the downfall of our courtship. I grew a solid pair of balls and questioned the shit out of him in the most curious yet friendly way possible and he was not buying any of it. Shit. He was smarter than I was. Or was he? Was he fuck! A family gathering where he adopted his "big man" approach to my parents' friend was the icing on the cake for my nerves. I was like who is this absolute moron?! Moreover, who am I for empowering his manipulating ass into thinking I am falling for his bullshit.

A mere few days later, he disappears off the radar of life. After going to his car sales job. Hardly a trip to the moon warranting radio silence but he went full silence mode meaning I naturally worried. For his safety, for my neediness but ultimately because I cared. He just chose the path of least resistance and completely shut me out. The analyzing and painful realization of just what was happening was awful at the time I can assure you. I had invested around 3 months into this courtship and looking back now, whilst I was smart and knew something was wrong; I did care for him. For the idea of him anyway. Realizing now that I have grown as a person that his behavior was merely him protecting his truth. Whatever that is/was. It was not in my story that I was to know just how damaged he was or just how hard his own struggle was. Lord knows I cannot judge him too much as he was the reason for my smile on more than one occasion. But growth as a woman was far superior and my inner awareness was growing in strength day by day following this dip in my self-awareness and indeed dignity.

Not all was lost. Plenty of fish brought me some right beauties. From the person who could not contain his erectile awareness in public to the person who had a fascination with anal sex and it was the second question he asked about after my name of course. What the actual fuck?!

Is this the future I asked myself? Is my future life dictated by my awareness or lack thereof of my particular preferences in ass sex and the like? Holy shit. I was scared. HA.

Then there was Christian, an architect from Edinburgh, good looking, sexy, great banter and an incessant texter and communicator. Could not wait to meet him. Could this be my shot? Fuck no. Biggest catfish around. I quickly realized he was not an actual person. Not as bad as robot life but the fact he always had an excuse to not meet me soon became clear when Nev Schulman launched his show 'Catfish' which depicted tales of two star-crossed lovers who meet online, chat for like 27 years and then eventually meet only because of the MTV craze of linking people who have not met. With a catch though. There is usually an abundance of lies and deceit on one side. Alternatively, the person is like a different gender than they say they are. Can you imagine? I was never to establish just what

Christian was but he was absolutely magnificent and keeping up a momentum of being an actual person. I believed his shit for a period of time, until I was losing my fucking patience falling hard for what could be a 65-year-old serial killer who sat in his pants masturbating at my selfies. Fuck the fuck off my friend.

Ah the tales of Plenty of fish they are a plenty. I could write an entire book on my internet dating degree. I have paid my dues and gained my masters that I am certain of! However, I will not. Not because I cannot be assed and this book is more than enough for now BUT because who needs to be reminded in 200 pages of failed shots at romance that they are destined to be the proud owner of a 50-year-old bachelorette studio and the mother of 16 cats? Me.

Five whole years had passed since Mark and I had split. I hadn't experienced anything remotely long term and whilst I wasn't in any hurry to marry off and live the white picket fence life; I was curious to know if I would ever feel that safety net again. You know that feeling of knowing you belong to someone. You are someone's someone. I missed that greatly and it obviously reaped from my pours when speaking authentically and frankly about my love goals and inspirations.

Invited to contribute to the planning of my companies' sales conference the forthcoming summer was to act as a catalyst to me getting "stuck in" to my work and forgetting everything else that had happened in the past few months. In addition, Shirley leaving for a second time (HAHA), losing my brother to his own bitterness; and attracting and subtracting an absolute gem of a nut job in the New York saga; I was embracing a fresh challenge. Perhaps getting involved in some extracurricular work tasks would pave the way for future promotion? I was not sure but I knew I was ace at my job. And planning the Christmas parties (usually in Cardiff, what a riot and Nicola Saltman can vouch for that!) was my forte. They were the days' travel was cheap and the company did not care that us measly PA's travelled for a party! WOOP.

Anyway…Andy Rowson, my manager. What an absolute gem of a boss. Hired by him back in 2009 I have never been so thankful to work for a leader like him. Our working relationship was top notch. He will always be my favorite. He inspired me, encouraged me and praised me. He was the catalyst to me working that extra hard with hopes of doing something a bit more with my company…that day would eventually come…

First, the year of 2012 was the big 30. Holy shit, where had my life gone? It was only yesterday I was in the Butlins arcade spending my fiver wisely.
Adulthood had crept upon me like a smooth mother fucker. And I was embracing it to my fullest. Planning a 30th birthday party was a riot. Morag, Mum, my hero, was as always a planning machine. Adopting the "let me handle it" approach my only wish was for a cool handbag shaped cake. And of course for people to turn up. HAHA.

My best friends were equally excited for my excitement. Some friends could not attend. Some were on vacay or just stuffing their faces at home with a pizza. I was not judging. I picked my dress wisely. A nice lilac number. My love and appreciation of my hefty legs was yet to be discovered so for this party I did sport some rather questionable tights. Please do not judge me. They were extra shiny. Holy shit. And my eyebrows. For fuck sake, I had shady eyebrows. I now cringe every time September 15 comes around each year and Facebook reminds me of the "on the day" feature from years gone by. And I am reminded of my lack of make-up awareness. Contouring was not yet contemporary so it was a "winging" it approach to face changing. I was shit. In addition, fat. Nevertheless, my good mate Suzie McNair was on hand to gift me the greatest gift. Goonies inspired Chunk t-shirt. Who does not love the Goonies man? Best gift ever. I was delighted. There were gifts a plenty to come.

One of which was the mural of photos from my childhood taking up its royal position at the buffet station of my party. Fuck my life. Cringe central. Not only did I use to resemble a boy, I had zero awareness of just how ugly I was as a child. Even into my late 20's. Jesus, someone needed to have given me a lesson in style years ago. So there I am sporting lilac dress, shady tights, heluva set of eyebrows, and the party was in full swing. Icing on the cake that night was most definitely my sister singing a song for me.

Ashleigh, definitely one of the best singers I know. She belted out Caledonia like the pro she is. Stunning performance, which spiked the tears a plenty. Riot for my makeup I can assure you. Mhairi Kennedy, another bestie was on hand to console my drunken tears as I made my way around the party loving and adoring all my fans. It sure was heartwarming to see so many lovely people who came to celebrate with me. I was of course 'mongoosed' by the end of the night. DJ Mark Dunn was the highlight of the night playing my favorite disco dancing track Superstar by Jamelia…HOLLER! Fist pump. Could not walk in the shoes I bought for the occasion and my feet were an absolute riot come 2am but it was the best night ever.

Little did I realize that the event I assisted on a mere one day before my party was to pave the way for an invite to work on another event…?

And so my 30th year was off to a great start. Great friends, great gifts! Seriously good people in my life. Still a little residual insecurity around abandonment that contributed to my awareness of friends coming and going but overall I was feeling confidant in my life.

Decided to add to my brood of feline friends. My very good longtime friend Stephen and his beauty of a doll Dawn were offloading the litter of their lovely cat and had a ginger ninja on offer. Mine please. I wanted a kitten. I was yet to approach the subject with Toby.

He had been in charge in my home for a near 7 years by this point and I was being rather

ballsy arranging this adoption without so much as a conversation with him. He was

guaranteed to lose his shit I could feel it coming.

However, this little ball of ginger cuteness was too much for words. I had him reserved

and named before he was even 2 weeks old. I did have to wait a little longer for him to be

trained etc. but the countdown was on my friends. Approached the subject with Toby. You

remember Toby right. *The only constant male in my life.* Never caused any tears. Well

apart from the day he ripped my leg when I tried to force him to hug me. Coz I am a needy

cow remember. He hated that shit.

Ginger ninja was to be known as Calvin. As in Calvin Harris, Armani pants model and

Scottish DJ extraordinaire.

Calvin was to join my clan, piss all over my nice white 1200 thread Egyptian cotton bed

sheets within 5 minutes of me getting him home meanwhile Toby loses his rag, rips my

new suit jacket and hides in my wardrobe hissing at first glance of Calvin and I wasn't

even in from work 3 minutes. What a joyous night that was.

That was until I discovered that Calvin was a girl. Howling.

Renamed to Calla I was the proud owner of a boy and a girl. Who needed a man? Not me.

I had two cats, a happy group of friends and Ann Summers finest economical rabbit for

working girls on the go. Man I was a happy vibrating little camper.

Then I met John Urbanik. What a gem of a person. Clearly had his own shit going on but his rustic silver fox look was to die for. Banter a plenty and some key skills (wink wink) he brought some romantic joy to my life for a good few months and I am pleased to report that we are still friends to this day, even though our romantic paths were not destined for longevity.

Funny how people cross your path is not it? They come, they go, they stay, they flow. Strongly believing that our lives are already planned for us I tried to embrace a more carefree approach to just breathing and letting things be. Without being too critical of myself, I allowed life to take its course. There were some things that were on my list of "fix now or forever hold your peace" and one of them was the need to address my diet. And exercise approach.

Decided to take on Just Dance. The Wii craze dance game and a new Beyoncé was surely going to be born eh? Emmm not quite. But a tidy bonus from work and a trip to Turkey was as sure-fire incentive to get the weight off.

Harder than I imagined. Was not a success. I just loved my food too much. I casually put my comfort eating down to growing but at 30 years old, that mantra was about 20 years out of date. HAHA.

However, a new chapter refocus was about to come my way in the form of a call from the top boss at my work when DJ called to ask if I would like to work on Top Achievers.

Top Achievers, a company recognition program celebrating the success of top performing staff by rewarding them with a trip to a location in the world that was yet to be established.

I was asked to work on the project. If there was ever a moment of pride in my career it was that defining moment of self-awareness. To have inspired a senior manager to entrust me with the responsibility of working on such an amazing event was life changing. I was thrilled. Karen Rome, the events manager for my company was a joy of a person to work with. Having worked under her remit a few times in the previous years I knew this was my chance to prove myself.

My first question, what is the location this year DJ. "Where is it"? "It is in ABU DHABI".

Oh holy fuckballs baby Jesus lord and master. Where the actual fuck is Abu Dhabi? Is that Dubai I asked? God love me. "Yes Mel it is in the United Arab Emirates".

Wowser. My passport had only ever been westernized and now it was about to get all ARAB up in itself.

Ok, so, I have this outstanding task of working on Achievers, I actually get to go on the trip and I am to be prepared to get a whole 3 hours sleep the entire time I am there. Sign me up Mohammed! ☺

With a whole 4 months until departure, I have a multitude of work to complete before then. I have regular meetings to attend on theme, winners, planning, spending; worshipping the ground my working world and Duncan Jarrett walk on for all I thought about those months was Abu Dhabi. Feeling as if I belonged to something was and insane and awe inspiring feeling. Being capable of completing such a task and not disappointing did undoubtedly cause a little unnecessary pressure on me but nothing my inner champion could not handle with sheer finesse.

I genuinely could not wait. Planning such an amazing experience for someone else to enjoy is so very liberating. From the filming of the winners' reactions when they were told to the planning of the themes, the tour guides, the flights and hotel bookings to the weekly meetings brain dumping and buzzing about the schedule was keeping me entirely motivated and inspired by travel. I was convinced I was irritating the shit out of all my mates because I genuinely think it was all I as capable of talking about for about 3 months and I was not even an achiever myself. LOL.

I felt supremely confidant and proud of my skills. I thrived at planning and discussing just how my contribution would benefit the entire program as it gave me hope that I had indeed found my calling. Was I about to completely change the face of my career? Was this meant for me all along? Was I meant to travel the world and see the Middle East? Was I meant for a chapter change…?

14

Start spreading the

news

2013 started with a bang.

I was preparing for the biggest working trip/event of my life; I was feeling excited and nervous at the same time AND I was free of a working issue that had been long overdue. I was focused on Abu Dhabi and all its planning in addition to realizing that I was just not pulling off the peroxide look anymore. I mean honestly…my hair was so blonde and bright the sun was depressed!

Dyed it dark brown and packed my case for the "Dhabs". Not before discovering a new show called Nashville. Nashville, a fiction based series focusing on country singers and their lives in Nashville, Tennessee. Brilliant and the music amazing. Trying to not convince myself I was destined to be a star on the country scene was a task in itself. My sister and I regularly discussed the series as the episodes went by.

And the day arrived. Abu Dhabi Top Achievers 2013 was upon me. The gathering of all the Achievers and their loved ones at Edinburgh Airport was a riot. Everyone was in the bar. Typical Scottish start to a holiday. I had of course already had the pleasure of witnessing most of them being told they had won and of course had befriended a few in preparation. More so, they knew I was their go-to and they could ask me anything. I was not an achiever in the sense of the concept of the program but I certainly felt like an achiever that day. Rounding everyone up at Edinburgh airport in preparation for the flight to Manchester to spend it overnight. Then flying out the following morning direct to Abu Dhabi with Etihad airways. Keeping everyone in check was fine. I was just as excited as they were. Some of the achievers had never been to the Middle East, some had never won anything and some had never realized they were deserving of such an award. It truly was awe inspiring to watch these amazing colleagues realize their recognition right from the get go. It was all systems go. They would want for nothing. Their rooms, flights, mini bar spend, evening meals, allowance, trips, sunshine and tan were all free. It was the crème-de-la-crème of holidays.

Moreover, we were to stay in the world-renowned Emirates Palace. A 7-star wonder of the Middle East and we were not to be disappointed.

Upon arrival at Abu Dhabi Airport, Karen was already on sight with the Photographer snapping up arrival reactions from the achievers. Some were like oh hell no! Having flown for like 8 hours it was fair to say there was bed head all round, including mine. My contact lenses were stuck to my eyeballs but I was programming myself to go into work mode immediately for I had a job to do. Top priority was impressing DJ with my skills.

I do not think I have ever seen such a beautiful building upon arrival at the Palace. The palatial grounds, the exquisite fountains, the grand entrance and the detailed finish absolutely astounded me so I can only imagine how the achievers must have felt.

For DJ to have mastered this entire program and executing a vision of reward was truly inspiring from the point of view of employee. I really respected his contribution to empowering and motivating his top achievers.

Check in was slick and smooth. Now I would be lying if I said I was not desperate to hit the hay after a long soak in the tub BUT arrival drinks in the BBQ-Al-Qasr outdoor gondolas of the Palace was on the agenda first.

Not before we were escorted to our rooms to drop a few things off. Oh my fucking baby Jesus and lord above. What a room. As Kit quoted in Pretty Woman, "my bathroom was bigger than the blue banana". It was. I quickly emptied my suitcase only to refill it immediately in a sweeping motion with the entire contents of the bathroom; of which there were plenty. The products alone were a month's mortgage! I was like a fat kid on cake day. Remember "lardass" from Stand by Me (the film) when he is triumphant in the pie eating contest? Well he was my inspiration in the bathroom-sweeping contest. The bed, the view, the fresh fruit, the grandness and the décor just blew my tiny mind. At this point though my eyes were like piss holes in the snow after a 24-hour marathon travel; event management and not fucking up my one task of getting everyone there in one piece.

Therefore, drinks overlooking the water were on the agenda. Everyone was welcomed and the drinks started to flow. I was excited for the achievers I really was. Karen and I checked out our allocated event room and were introduced to the onsite events manager so that our queries could be dealt with efficiently.

Our amazing photographer Matt was on point to establish a running photo-documented commentary on large plasma daily. We were to ask the achievers to come to the event room each morning at a specific time so the day could begin. Karen was a complete machine in efficiency. With adjoining rooms and an abundance of collateral already shipped to the UAE in advance, we were a well-oiled machine…dream team.

Matt was the icing on our cake. He was going to help us truly remember the memories and I was to thoroughly enjoy working with him. Albeit the most exhausting task to handle! And so day 1 was over. Finally, Bed time bedtime bedtime. Shower, Skype, dance like Beyoncé in my pants in preparation for waking to the most humid and scorching heat in arguably the nicest hotel I had ever been in. Not to mention work my ass off. Literally. My ass was worked so much I lost like five kilograms that entire trip.

Day two. Sun rose. Call time 630am. Holy fuck. I set two alarms just to be safe. Oh my actual god if my eyes were not bad on day 1 they were certainly horrific on day 2. Enjoyed a superb breakfast before rounding up the troops for a trip to the heritage center and an evening at Pearls and Caviar, a top restaurant booked exclusively for us.

The day just flew by. Flying by the seat of my grannie pants became second nature. I was sweating like an absolute beast but we did manage to ride a camel and get some amazing selfies Karen and me. It was incredible. I did not really feel like I was working in the corporate sense of the word, more just assisting an amazing group of people who were already enjoying themselves to the fullest.

I remember having a brief conversation with Julie Barlas, Customer Service winner for 2012, on the TA program with her husband Craig. "I am having the time of my life Mel". The sincerity and appreciation in her eyes was stunning. She was incredibly thankful to my company and to her colleagues for nominating her. The exhaustion I felt was drowned by a wholehearted warm feeling of contentment. This was what life was all about. Watching people enjoy. Not thinking or over analyzing but just enjoying.

The days turned into nights and soon the extravaganza of the Top Achievers awards day arrived. Call time was stupid o'clock and DJ's right hand man Chris, an all-round AV masterpiece of skills was on point to transform the Emirates Palace ballroom into the event of the decade. Absolute mayhem so it was. From table settings, to drapes, to stage set up, to run through, to arrival etiquette, to positioning of photographer, to run through of itinerary, to speech prep, to DJ losing his shit if he didn't have a constant supply of red bull to the miraculous speed at which my heart was racing to get everything right. This was going to be a compounding night in peoples' life for we were to display colleagues talking openly about how each achiever was deserving. A film was played, focusing on each achiever as their respective video was played and they were welcomed to the stage to collect their awards. As I sit and write this in 2016, I still feel immense emotion reliving the joy that was that night. The look on their faces when they see how valued they were to the respect DJ commanded when he performed his opening act of getting around everyone quick smart and shaking their hands whilst the introductory song played. Everything timed to perfection. My duties were simple. Escort each achiever at my side of the room to the stage entrance and they will walk on and have their moment of fame. You laugh I get it. I laugh too. But it was a big deal to these amazing people. It was heartwarming to watch.

Every achiever had their moment in the limelight and it was only fitting that I was a big ball of emotion being wrapped up in the awe of it all.

Then DJ did the unthinkable. A real moment of pride for me.

He thanked all the achievers for their efforts and then went onto say he had one more thank you. To someone who had gone the extra mile working long hours and contributing fully to the planning and success of the event; Me.

"This girl has worked tirelessly, sometimes behind the scenes and gone over and above her duties. I want to thank her for her outstanding efforts and would like to welcome Mel to the stage". Proudest moment of my life. I remember Julie Clapperton sitting at the table in front of me looking around to acknowledge she knew he was referring to me before I knew it. Tears filled my eyes and I had to try to keep it together and not fall on my face walking up the stairs. Even though I had rehearsed that walk, all day long, my legs were like jelly, I could feel my tears welling up in my eyes as DJ, and Karen awaited me on the stage. Presenting me with a token of thanks, I was filmed and photographed in my truest form of inner happiness. I can count on one hand my most memorable times and this was one of them.

I felt like all the past hurt, disappointment, feelings of pain and sorrow and soul searching had diminished only to be replaced by this tranquil moment of pride and self-satisfaction. The night was then in full swing. I was allowed a glass of wine. At that moment in time, I could have easily downed a triple vodka valium latte but alas, the Chianti was on offer so I tanned that before I called it a night. The party went on into the wee hours and of course, I could not switch off so changed and went back down. Exhaustion had been royally replaced by exhilaration and an abundance of energy. I was off down to dance the night away.

Little did I know the party was already over and the hotel team already dismantling the entire room BUT there was wine left of the tables. So seeing as I reined supreme in the "Sweeping of unnecessary shit" Olympics I went around lifting up all the leftover red wine bottles and myself, Chris and Karen had ourselves a little party in a dark corner of the palace. That is until security said we had to leave. Probably because we were bringing down the esteem of the hotel looking like a group of homeless people ready to pass out. Which I was of course. However, I was to only have around 3 hours sleep before the next days' events were to take place. Thankfully, it was to be considered a rest day and I was to get 2 hours' free time.

What does a 30-year-old single woman do with 400 pounds of spends she has yet to spend and has 2 hours of free time? You got it, eat, pray and shop. Shop I did. I was like a contestant on supermarket sweep given time and money and told to spend like an absolute demon. Spend I did. Marina mall was a mere 10-dirham ride away of which I was to claim

back LOL! 2 hours of absolute bliss buying clothes, candles, and make up and shit I did

not need.

Then returning to the hotel for the last nights' festivities. An outdoor BBQ. Outstanding.

The whole experience had now resonated with every achiever. They felt motivated, they

felt appreciated and together we made some beautiful memories. We were in full swing

that night smoking shisha, eating delicious seafood, enjoying a sunset and beautiful views

of the gulf. We had an early rise for departure but for me my journey was not over. Setting

aboard the bus to the airport, I felt great sadness. A sweeping feeling of regret almost.

Regret for what I wondered? I soon realized it was not regret. It was hope. Could my life

be a life in Abu Dhabi? How? Where? In what capacity? It was a moment of clarity that

required further investigation…

Not before landing back in Scotland to absolute shit show of pissing down rain. I mean

honestly. I sporting my finest flip-flops (which I still do when I travel home nowadays no

matter the season!) and the rain was horrific. My very good friend Fiona Simpson

collected me at the airport because she is indeed a wee sausage. And I am finding it hard to

even converse for I am an absolute mess. I need to sleep for like 3 days! Therefore, I get to

my flat, sans cats for they are still in the cattery thank fuck! I put on my electric blanket

(bear in mind it is March and Scotland sees summer weather one day a year on average!)

and shower for what seems an eternity. Then climbing into my onesie and switch my lights

off and I drift off into a state of resting bliss. No alarm, day off work and I sleep for 19

hours. Al Hamdulilah.

Back to work and the buzz about achievers is rife. Some postproduction work is in full

flow; photo editing, production of memory digital photos for the Achievers and an extensive catch up on all my emails ensued. That is until Matt shared the photos of the trip, of which I am in a singular picture. And the dread that I have been denying myself becomes all too real. I am overweight. I look dreadful, unhealthy and its really just my smile and my good heart that are my finest features.

It was a revelation. I broke down in front of my mum (Morag, not Hitlers army!) and she promised to help me completely change my diet and lifestyle.

No more Chinese, no more takeaways, no more excessive portions and not doing anything remotely near enough to burn it all off. Why was my diet the previous year not a success? Because I clearly did not want it enough.

This time it was different. Not only did I want to look good for me, I wanted to look good for the new life I had now paved out for myself.

I was going to be healthy and I was going to emigrate to the Middle East.

Just how I was going to pull that off was beyond me like but I had a vision.

I started running. Daily behind my flat in Camelon. Just along the canal and back each morning totaling around 3.8km. Sporting new trainers by Nike I was feeling spectacular in my awesome attire. I was shit at running and out of breath most runs but I was trying. And Toby joined me on occasion.

I started taking regular shots of my body. In the mirror so I could monitor the difference. The change to my diet was drastic. I bought enough supplies for each week and ensured I had breakfast and lunch prepped. Having dabbled in vegetarianism for around 1 year I was back on the meat. Meat was a necessity.

After 3 weeks, I was over one stone down. I was feeling epic. Wednesday was weigh day. I was so determined. I had no external group supporting me I was just eager to accomplish this alone, with the aid of my mum. I kept a regular dialogue with her and my friends. I was undoubtedly the most irritating social media blogger in those initial months as I was constantly in search of online support just to give me that ego boost I needed to keep going. So I did not lose momentum and have to admit I would forever be a failing fatty. My legs were starting to tone. I was using my Wii fit board to weigh and monitor my loss. There is no greater feeling that the Wii mii (your Wii character) shrinking each times you stand on the board. Watching the weekly graph go downwards was motivation in itself. Rain or shine I was trotting along that canal knowing the day would come I would buy a smaller size in clothes.

To know my friends and loved ones were pleased to see my whole outlook on life change I was feeling really confidant and self-aware. Which completely transformed any residual anxiety or worry I had about menial issues in day-to-day life?

Do not get me wrong I was still shit at dating and keeping the cats from kicking the shit out of each other but I had order in my routine and my body was changing.

Buying a size 12 in skinny jeans was a triumphant moment for me. Only 3 months in was three stone down almost. My clothing budget was near to zero so I had to improvise and start cutting and threading my own clothes to fit. But boy did I feel wonderful. Taking a selfie for my friends' birthday party in front of the mirror and seeing how small my waist and my ass had become made me cry with excitement. I finally felt sexy. In addition, having gone full circle from my days of being bullied for being less than pretty, I sure felt I had accomplished the right to two-finger salute those sorry fuckers who said I would never be attractive. On that particular day of mirror hugging I ruled the world. Saying to myself, "I win". Fuck you haters.

Summer of festival loving and hobo chic fashion was upon us. Not before my sister gave birth to my beautiful nephew Harvey, a surprise baby but a beautiful baby I was thrilled to have the pleasure of helping her deliver. Named after my Nana's maiden name it was a fitting tribute to her. I was so proud of Ashleigh on that day.

My diet and regime was reigning supreme. I was excited to countdown to T in the Park, Scotland's answer to Woodstock. Without the hippie love. Instead it is cans of tenants and overcrowded toilet cabins that have not seen anti-bacterial wipes since Jesus was a boy. But a lineup to die for. From Calvin Harris to Killers, to Rudimental to Ellie Golding; Mhairi, and myself my most awesome bohemian soul sister took on the epic T arena like tramps on chips. Armed with a vodka or 12 we befriended some lovely English girls and some epic memories were made. Mhairi, a childhood friend of my sisters but now a friend of mine was one of those rare acquaintances who I would never have imagined would become one of my very best friends; had an ability to completely calm my mind. A reiki master she had a supreme talent of rationalizing any irrational thoughts and the icing on the cake being we had the same love for Rudimental, the band. Who wouldn't love that type of kindred love? I love her very being.

I feel I grew a lot closer to all my friends during that particular summer. Whilst were all in separate places doing bits and pieces, I truly felt connected to them. Having been friends with Sam for so many years on a continuous year on year friendship she was my closest soldier sister. Sharing a surname, we often pretended and still do pretend we are family. Fitting to be honest because she will always be my family. She just lived a bit of a distance from me. Being based in Falkirk and working in Edinburgh meant planning was essential to meet up. Suzie lived in London so I never seen her but we chatted all the time.

Then there was Gael, the Pricey, Price. An absolute gem. She introduced me to Carly and Marcella, two awesome weegies who just brighten up anyone's life.

Not forgetting my very good friend Pamela. Having met Pamela in 2002 she was a constant. But she shied away from the social media life and that of getting out and about. Happy and content living the quiet life with her husband Alan I respected everything about her traditional vision and was happy for her. I just did not see her very often. I missed her.

Terribly. Nevertheless, life goes on, people move on, people evolve and people change. That is all ok. I forgave myself for feeling that way, as I could not spend my days over analyzing why we did not all live the exact same path.

I was feeling elated at this point of my life. I had great people around me, good things going on, work was great and DJ had asked me to work on the following year's achievers, which I of course was delighted to say yes to. My diet was going well, albeit plateauing a little due to a constant loss. This was expected but knowing my over active imagination I was of course thinking to myself do not get fat Melanie do not get fat! I was extra conscious of my eating habits. So much so if I went on a night out and had a cheeky takeaway on way home, I would most definitely feel guilt ridden and rock up at 7am for a hike along the canal or jog to Stirling. I did this on the day Andy Murray made the Wimbledon final and won. God bless his determination. If there is ever a determined athlete, it is he. Cannot say the same for myself on that day. Absolutely hanging out my arse with a hangover from hell and I have the remnants of cold pizza on my bed. I trotted the whole 16km to Stirling. I was dead set of ridding myself of the guilt of being a cheeky muncher at 2am. Little did I realize it was so hot I was burnt silly. But Mama Hume had an epic feast awaiting me on this beautiful summer's day. And Murray won his first Wimbledon grand slam. That was a special moment for Scotland. It is just a pity out of all the hot tennis players we got the one who never cracks a smile. Bless him.

Therefore, summer was in full swing. A chance conversation with my very lovely colleague Suzanne was to pave the way for a little injection of love in my life. Which I probably needed at that point.

Suzanne introduced me to Colin. Colin was a very handsome and charming roofer from Tranent, Edinburgh. A cheeky sort with banter that could get you out your knickers in 2.5 seconds...

Ahem, first dates are never easy but meeting him was natural. We had such a lovely time. He was sexy and funny. Tall and lean but very manly. Just what the doctor ordered. I really enjoyed his company and immediately found him attractive enough to meet my cats. LOL

Our conversation resembled that of a love story I will not lie. What we discovered in terms of common interests and appreciation of same tastes really compounded our courtship. My parents liked him and whilst I did have some reservations about him being a dad to two daughters by two different women, I would be lying if I said that even became an issue. It never did. All he had to do was be himself. And he was. He was very attentive. He made me feel special, loved, and attended to. We spoke for hours on end about life, our dreams, our ambitions, our families, our values and our desire to be together. Spending time with his family was also lovely. Then meeting his daughters was special to. Granted he did have some flaws, we all do. I was no picnic and can be quite demanding and needy but it really is just because I do not want to give away too much free of charge when it should be appreciated. However, he always made me feel appreciated. He had innate dad values. He adored his kids and that reminded me of my dad. So I had a soft spot for the goodness of his heart. And his love for his family was ever evident. He was protective and cared for me. I felt loved. For the first time in a long *long* time and since Mark in 2006, 2013 seen me fall in love for just the second time in my life. I could see him and I having a future together. We even talked openly about how happy we felt together and I felt elated. I was blinded by love. I saw no wrong in him. I never questioned him at all in any sense and trusted him fully. That did scare me slightly but I could not imagine my life without him. It is amazing how one person can completely transform your life to the point that life prior to them becomes slightly faded. Looking back, I like to call that a phase of perspective. I had a vision of tranquil and content family living and it resonated well in my overall dreams to settle. I wanted to fall in love and I could feel myself falling for him. He was on my mind constantly and we grew so close. I loved his touch, his hugs, his presence and his chat. He stimulated me in many ways and it was highly refreshing.

He was my Prince Charming. Just the ghetto kind as he had swag. But he loved me. I could feel it. You know how you can just feel it. Well I felt it. It swept my conscience like a wave of emotion every waking moment of every waking day.

I thought I had found the love of my life. My heart was whole.

And then one day a call came that changed everything…

The Final Chapter

What is the script?

There are phone calls and there are phone calls. You purposely avoid the ones from your bank, the electricity company and the companies wanting to sell you double-glazing but you most definitely answer the calls or the CALL from the key to your future kingdom. Wouldn't you? I very nearly missed answering the call but the +971-country code was too enticing to avoid. And boy was I glad I did.

Forgetting that upon return from Abu Dhabi in March I registered my rather mediocre CV on Gulf Talent.com, little did I know that recruiters actually use these sites to source talent. Who knew? No me obviously!

I am sitting at my desk on 23 August 2013 and its 12.20pm. Picture this. Sitting there not even glancing in my phones direction and it starts buzzing. +971… That is the UAE. I knew it because of our work trip so I was of course curious. Then fear initially set upon me because I thought oh shit we have not paid a bill and now they are chasing me. I answer.

"Hello"

"Hello, is that Melanie Hume"

"Yes, speaking"

"Hi Melanie, my name is Bal and I work for a company called Adecco in Dubai. We are interesting in speaking to you about a position in Abu Dhabi".

"Sorry, what"

"A position in Abu Dhabi, the United Arab Emirates".

"Emm, ok"

"Can I tell you a bit about the position?"

"Emm, yes of course".

Yes, you fucking can my friend!!!

I am sitting there at my desk with, what can be described as a surprised expression across my face. My colleagues are looking at me like who the actual f.u.c.k is she talking to so naturally I have to get up and move away before I spontaneously combust into a screaming mess of excitement that a company in Dubai/Abu Dhabi/somewhere hot, want to talk to me. Talk to Melanie Hume, a Personal Assistant from Scotland. Little old Scotland.

Of course, I adopt my corporate poker face telephone etiquette so that I dazzle this Bal with my outstanding greatness. Meanwhile I am thinking to myself just how the actual fruck a duck have they found me. Do not fuck this up Melanie I am saying to myself.

So we discuss in detail my working life. Standard. A PA is a PA. However, how you execute your talent is something only a great PA knows how to articulate. So I go into detail but in a summarizing manner because I quickly establish he is writing it all down in preparation to introduce me to a company employee, presumably HR. He asks if I know the region and if I have had exposure…of which I can confidently say absolutely my friend. Abs-fucking-lutely.

At this point in the conversation, my very good friend Lesley, who worked in risk, walks past me and looks at me curiously and I cannot resist the urge to quickly scribble down a few words…

"There is a company in Abu Dhabi who want and need an assistant…they want me"

Holy shit. Shit just got real. Her eyes widen with hope and faith in me. I loved her for that. Always so encouraging to my skills and me. She had previously been a huge catalyst for me seeking some mind coaching from her friend to overcome my grief of the Shirley era.

And so Bal, my new best friend from Adecco Dubai is rabbiting on about who, where, how, what, package, life, culture, relocation!

"Are you interested?"
"Yes Bal, I believe I really am".
"Ok what I need to do now is set up a telephone interview with the HR recruiter for the company"
"Yes absolutely happy for that to take place"
"And you are definitely open to relocating from the UK to the UAE"
"Yes Bal, absolutely".

OH. MY. GOD.

This was my dream. To work for a successful banker, in the beautiful city of Abu Dhabi, surrounded by the culture and life I had very quickly become fond of and accustomed to. Could I make this my life? Could I make the move on my own to a completely different country? A country I have only had minimal exposure to? Could I take a risk and work for someone I have never met?

The call was scheduled with Claire, a recruiter for the bank. The countdown to that day was painful. Oh lord it was longwinded and torture waiting to impress someone enough they want to essentially change my entire life. No pressure.

And the day came. Prepared with stats on lifestyle, culture, company background and values and of course, a detailed researched synopsis of who would become my boss I was ready for her.

The phone rang. I answered and she fired questions at me rapid style. I responded in true confidant and corporate style. It would either serve me well or diminish my chances if I was perceived to be arrogant or cocky. Which I never ever want anyone to view me as. However, some peoples' perspective can rapidly change with choice of wording and tone of voice. I was keen to avoid that at all costs. I wanted her to believe she had found the person they needed.

It was a success. I was asked to make time to speak to their senior. A seasoned banker, Simon, British and well established as an expert in his field. A man I knew of but did not know personally. A Skype would be arranged for the coming Thursday at 7pm my time. 10pm UAE time. They were 3 hours ahead. Most nerve-wracking build up to a call. And it was to be by Skype.

Speaking of Skype. My Skype name at that point was "Melaniexxx"…a name Bal said resonated with a porn star so that had to change quick smart. So I changed it.

Went and got my nails done just to distract me and I could not contain my excitement so ended up telling my nail technician just what my plans for that night were! I must have been a riot. Nevertheless, I bet I endeared anyone who stood in my path that day/week. For the elation, filling my veins must have been evident to all and sundry.

My iPad was set, I was prepared with a detailed synopsis of just how bloody wonderful I was and how I would change his life.

He needed a detail orientated efficient Executive Assistant to come on board and sort his shit out. And sort his shit out was my main aim in selling my skills to him!

The Skype rang. I answered. He had clearly had a busy week but he was the most endearing man I had spoken to. And I had met a few amazing leaders in my time. He was specific in his needs and was blunt enough to be clear enough about what he did not want in an EA. I immediately felt that not only would this be a job I would enjoy; it would be a job I would excel in. I knew it in the depths of my conscience. This was meant for me. I did my very best to be articulate enough that he knew I was able to adapt and evolve with a huge change of culture, lifestyle and employer which of course would overwhelm the strongest of people. That was a certainty.

The call lasted around 30 minutes but it felt like it went by in a heartbeat. Then it was over. Did he like me, did I like him, could I move my entire life for him? Could I work for him? Would I survive life in the Middle East, was I ready to be an ex-pat?

I knew it was right. I could feel it in my bones. All my years of wondering if I belonged or if I fell into this line of work became clear. My path was written for me. I was ready for this. I was a success. I deserved this as much as the next person and he would not find anyone willing to work harder than me proving my worth and value.

The weekend came and went. Knowing that UAE working hours are Sunday to Thursday I had anticipated that feedback, if any, would likely come on the Sunday.

I remember that very day. Going to meet Fiona at Jam Jar, Bridge of Allan, for Sunday brunch, where by the way Judy Murray walked in for her Sunday coffee, I took the call of all calls. My heart burst with anticipation. It was Bal.

"Mel, they are moving to offer"

Writing that very statement above now, nearly 3 years later I still get Goosebumps thinking about it.

"They are verbally offering you the position pending sign off of an offer of employment".

"They hope to have the written offer within one week"

Sunday 7th September 2013, happiest moment of my life. On the weight of a telephone chat and a Skype call, I was the person they wanted.

Being the day of the German Grand Prix (I think!), I knew my dad would be at home. Watching. Obsessing. He was the person I always wanted to tell good news to. I took a quick detour to my parents' house on way to meet Fiona. I fluffed a reason for my lateness, as I also wanted her to basque in my happiness by explaining to her in person.

My dad, sitting watching the grand prix happy as Larry never took his eyes off the screen when I sat down and said I had something to tell him.

"Dad, I have something to tell you"
"Yes"
"I have been offered a job in Abu Dhabi. I am going to take it and move there"
"There is a Grand Prix in Abu Dhabi Melanie, well done my darling".

Result. If there is a grand prix he is a happy man. He glanced at me with his eyes. His proud eyes. His smile widened and I knew at that moment I had made him prouder than he had ever been. Of my strength and me.

I wanted to tell my mum personally but she was over at Ashleigh's and I had to go meet Fiona. So I told my dad not to tell her and that I would pop in later to tell them both. Oh how the joy was written all over my person. I was so happy. So thrilled.

Told Fiona. We had a joyous fist pump and boobie hug.

Then took a call from a lovely woman calling on behalf of Simon, from the same bank. Simon had kindly asked her to call me to familiarize me with life in the UAE and offer a friendly connection. A connection I would later thank him for because she was a huge help in introducing me to UAE life.
This wonder was Kate Mated. An English rose with a beautiful accent, clearly educated and smart. She was a joy to speak to. Offering her assistance in finding me a good nail salon and yoga studio, I knew I had found a friend and a huge support before I had even left Scotland.

Written offer had yet to arrive. Of course, I am trying to keep calm but telling everyone who would listen takes over my ability to just calm my disco pants.

T-7 days until that letter arrived.

Longest 7 days. I had to tell Colin. Remember Colin. My life, my love, my darling. He was blissfully unaware. He needed to know. It was the least I could do. Be honest. Give him the option. I never wanted to exclude him from the process. I had to make it clear I was not asking him to ask me to stay. Far from it. I had to be honest with him that I wanted to go. What that would mean for us was something he would have to seriously consider.

Only once I had finished with my darling Fiona I had the exciting task of sharing it with my mum. She already knew I had a call but it was not really a reality until I sat her down and said, "They have offered me the job". Oh my word, if I ever had any doubt up until that point in my life about her love and adoration for me as her daughter; it was that defining moment of pride. She started to cry. I started to cry, my sister started to cry and together we celebrated this momentous change for me. For the better. For my future.

I could not sleep that night. I needed to tell Colin. I felt extreme guilt, as I knew it would be change for us. I also toiled with it being bad timing and consequential of life and all its turbulence.

He came over on the Monday and I told him. He was genuinely pleased for me. I was taken aback that he had such a selfless reaction. I expected him to immediately think of what that meant for him. He took himself out the equation and immediately tried to calm me. Reassure me it was an opportunity I could not turn down. An opportunity he was supportive of. How that was to affect our relationship was secondary. It did not faze him. I do not think I loved him more than I did at that moment. He was the definition of supportive love, friend, partner and soul mate. I felt comfort. Like it would all work out and it did not matter if we did not have a plan. This was unlike me. Especially at this heightened time of change.

The coming days were hard. I was incredibly run down and poorly. The realization of what was happening really hit me. My immune system was lacking vitamin C and the anticipation of receiving the offer in writing was really eating at me. I would be lying if I said I did not worry they would suddenly change their minds and withdraw the offer. I even went to the lengths of calling Bar for reassurance and he was like Mel, calm down its ok. The signatory is travelling but we will get it for you ASAP.

It was the countdown to birthday, September 15. Colin took me shopping. Spent a fortune on me and sent me off to Glasgow to enjoy a night with my girls.

My best friend, Sam went to great lengths to organize a unicorn cake. I was sporting my new dress Colin bought me and I had new extensions and lashes on. I was feeling foxy. It was the eve of my 31st birthday and life was amazing. I had amazing friends celebrating and loving me. I had a job offer, which meant a huge change for me, and I had a supportive family who just advocated my every move. I was blessed.

Waking up on Sunday 15 September 2013 with a hangover was less than present. However, stuffing my face with unicorn cake was redemption in itself.

Seeing my phone light up with Bal was the finest gift sent from God. My offer had been approved and the company was sending it directly to me. I was to check it, sign it and celebrate it.

Immediately upon receipt of the email of all emails I took another call from +971, a beautiful Arabic voice greeted me; a woman who would become a great friend to me; Yasmin, Recruiter for the bank, calling to congratulate me and answer any of my initial questions.

Explaining the entire relocation process, she immediately reassured me all was going to be ok. She even went so far as to say they were delighted I was joining their family. I was thrilled.

As were my friends. It was a life changing moment. It all became real. I called my mum and dad immediately. To confirm it was happening. No longer a tentative; now a definitive evolution of Melanie from Scottish sausage to desert princess.

Then I called Colin. Hardest conversation of my life. To break the news to my love that something verbal was now becoming a reality was hard. I could feel his sadness through the phone. I went to him. I needed to be with him. I needed to comfort him. He was a hanging mess of a hung-over wreck right enough and I was a bit pissed at him because it wasn't how I wanted to spend my birthday but I knew it wasn't easy news to hear. To hear your girlfriend is leaving the country was hardly music for his soul.

We spent the night together. On my birthday. The most memorable of birthdays.

The days and weeks to come would be a whirlwind. Nevertheless, Colin was a constant. A supportive backbone during a time of adjustment for me. I was arguably temperamental with overwhelming feelings of wonder and he was an absolute gem.

Resigning from my beloved company came with praise for my accomplishments and me. I was delighted and proud. DJ was also proud. He was the first person I told before I submitted my resignation.

Celebrations were a plenty that night. Of course, I took to Facebook to share my joy. And what momentous supportive words of encouragement I received from over 150 people. I felt liberated.

The four-week countdown to my one-way ticket to the desert was upon me.

Having a list as long as my arm of things to do was astounding. Priority was re-homing my beloved cats. Hardest goodbye ever. Toby, who I had had since he was a baby went to arguably the nicest girl I knew from the company. Such a warm soul. He is happy and still lives with her. That makes me happy.

Calla, the ginger ninja, was to go to my darling Fiona. She already had Callas sister Millie. So they would become a dream team.

Then came the task of shutting down my life. Tad dramatic I hear you say but that is how I surmised it in my mind. I had created this list of things to do. Speaking to the utility companies, cancelling my phone contract, paying off my student loans, trying to find a buyer for my car and my flat AND packing. How does one pack for a new life? I had a two case limit and it was like hell on earth choosing what to take and what not to take.
All the while Colin is constant. My friends are constant. My family is constant. It is just I that is an absolute neurotic riot of a mess.
Creating an Abu Dhabi folder was a joy though. I was researching everything from geography to the cost of a pint of milk to bank accounts to cool places to live.
The bank was being amazing and I was in constant contact with Simon.

Then the eve of my departure arrived. Wednesday 16th October was my last night in Scotland. Groomed for my new life I was settled but teary-eyed saying goodbye to my granddad. A lovely human being indeed. Saying goodbye to my sister and my niece and kissing my baby nephew goodbye. I was not sure at that moment when I would be coming home to visit; Christ I was not even sure I would like it!

Spending that last night with Colin was nostalgic. It was sad for both of us. We both knew this might pave the way for the end of our relationship and there was not much any of us could do. We had to trust fate would lead the way.

Never slept a wink.

My mum and dad took me to the airport.

My mum later said I never looked back when they waved me off into the security terminal. She was sad about that. What she did not know was I was holding back the tears. I did not want to turn around and see them cry. I needed to keep putting one foot in front of the other and keep going. I knew if I had turned around, I might not have gotten on the plane. It was hard walking away from my safety, my love and my life. Not knowing if the life at the other end was meant for me.

Landing in Abu Dhabi. I was overcome with emotion. Queuing at that eye scanning station is a sight for sore eyes I can assure you. Having flown through the night and looking like something out of shameless painted me in resting bitch face mode I was certain of it. However, my visa awaited, was stamped and I was here. I was home.

Being homed temporarily in a hotel was an absolute beauty. Weather was terrific. Landing on a Friday morning I did sleep for hours. Nevertheless, when I woke I decided to explore. It is like a fucking furnace outside right enough and I have clearly not put nearly enough sunscreen on for I was a burnt crisp within like 30 minutes. The room service, huge bed, huge TV and IPad were my friends. A bit like Wilson in the film Castaway with Tom Hanks. Except I did not talk to my iPad. I just talked to myself. All the time. I mean how long was it going to take to make pals? I am Scottish and a hoot, surely everyone wants to be pals with that? Right? Wrong.

This was to be a journey in itself. Making a new social circle. Wowser. However, I was prepared. I had overcome fear and anxiety about worse things so making friends was going to be a walk in the park...

NOT.

Work was a walk in the park. Any initial worry of being the new girl was quickly curbed by the insane workload awaiting me. Sorting out his life was my priority and I got to work quickly. I had to prove my worth. I had probation to get through.

I very quickly found my feet. It was amazing. Creating process and procedure that benefited Simon's office and the wider company was really quite something. Meeting Kate, being shown around the city from a resident perspective and receiving such incredible support from the staff at the bank was so appreciated.

I had 3 weeks in the hotel before I needed to move to my own place. I eventually found somewhere. Granted it required an open mind and a creative eye I set my sights on Ikea. Who doesn't love Ikea? Bought half the shop. Ok I bought the whole shop. But I had a great property owner who installed my TV on the wall AND built my furniture because clearly I was about as DIY friendly as a dead person. Not my forte. But I invited him to share a game of bowling and tennis on my Wii along with ice cream for desert. I am a lover not a fighter. First pal made. Well, after Kate. She was a gem.

And so my very first night out was planned. Halloween. Good job I had packed my Disney Minnie Mouse costume size 10 eh. Squeezing into that should be mentioned on my resume as a skill. It is like being on the crystal maze with no hope of winning a crystal but I look sexy when it is finally zipped up!

Welcomed by a rather intoxicated Australian biting my arm on the roof of what I can only describe at a frat house in Khalifa City was what I like to call my initiation to the Dhabs. Did I acquire some friends? Hell yes! Kate, her friend Dirms, Emi and of course the biting joker. He bruised me the asshole.

Brilliant night though. Ended up in a shithole of a nightclub though. I would later discover this but on that night I was the new girl in town sporting a cool costume and I had a strong desire to dance to the B52's love shack. Bring it. One of my fondest memories of my first few months in Abu Dhabi.

And of course I befriend all party goers on Facebook including the very lovely Louise Dewar and Jamie Craw. Who are both sitting in the corner of this party. What drew my attention to them you ask? Might it have been their outstanding accent? Scottish of course. Friendship immediately born. Winning.

Hangover central the following day. Argument with Colin. One of many. Sad times. The reality of a long distance relationship was becoming all too real and tiresome. On both of us. Albeit I loved every minute of our Skypes, it was not the same and I missed home. But I persevered.

Sorting out routing was priority. Getting a phone contract, a bankcard, a credit card, Christ getting a new pair of flip-flops was a chore. There is like 546 malls in Abu Dhabi. We are spoilt for choice.

Routine was a priority for me though. It re-established my control fixations. I needed to feel order, similar to the efficiency of running a calendar. I needed to feel contentment that I had everything under control.

I was clueless about any sort of ex-pat nightlife or indeed western gatherings. That was the toughest thing for me those first few months. I was not aware of etiquette, popular hang outs etc. It was only when Kate invited me to a brunch, a Friday gathering at many a UAE hotel where ex-pats, usually western, are gathering for a drinking and eating extravaganza; that I jumped at the thought of having new friends. Sign me up.

Got absolutely ringoed didn't I. Ended up taking multiple selfies with random people and mistaking this polish chick for Nicole Richie and making her highly uncomfortable whilst I tried to convince her she was famous. She was not and I was being a dick. HA.

It was on that day I met "the Colonel". The very charming Tom Calnan, a friend of Kates and leader of their imaginary army. Of which I was eager to join the cadets. The Colonel. What an absolute riot he is/was/will be.

A mutual interest in cats and a chance encounter with Emi, a girl I met at the Halloween party, introduced me to another group of people who then in turn introduced me the western brunch party scene, was to establish a bit more of a concrete circle. This pleased me no end. It unfortunately reinforced the distance between Colin and I.

I was feeling pretty lost. Loving my job and embracing this new way of meeting people by referral and by proxy was all very well but feeling like I was failing in my duties of loving someone who had my heart was tough on my conscience.

It was around that time that my best friend Sam Hume came to visit. Perfect timing. I clearly did not know even a fraction of the things I know now about popular haunts etc. so it was like the blind leading the blind us both touring the "Dhabs" And then her case did not arrive so carnage broke out and she went mental buying unnecessary shit including M&S bras (which was a necessity) LOL as my clothes were all too big for her! **monkey face**…

Having her with me was comfort in itself. She is real. She is so real she is a diamond of authenticity. Only stayed a few days but what a hilarious time we had. From getting burnt walking the corniche to getting shit faced in the Yacht Club. Hilarious weekend that. Had a screaming argument with Colin and it was obviously over. Just like that. I needed to move on. Whilst I was not sure if I was completely content in Abu Dhabi, I did know I had no burning desire to escape back to Scotland. I had to give my new life my full efforts and that is exactly what I did.

The coming months were hard and I was deeply lonely. I met some interesting people. One specifically, Jude. Lovely Scottish lady who was also a colleague. Her heartwarming welcome will always be appreciated.
I went to see the Rolling Stones, which was terrific. Managed to meet some new ex-pats through yet another brunch and some new friendships were born. Some have remained but some have expired. That is the ex-pat life.

We are not here to befriend everyone just because we are alone. Or are we? I do not think so. I have my best friends. I was looking for a replacement. I was looking for people to share my interests and perhaps find some common respectful ground.

Kate and I decided to join Tinder. Oh happy days. Tinder, the online gateway to a happy conclusion. If you are content with naked chat and a McDonalds milkshake.

I was inundated with potential matches. Tinder is like this playground of erotically charged boys who have never been allowed out of the playground before. Whilst it was initially addictive and food for your ego no less, the repetition of responding how you were and what you did for a living became tiresome and dull. Even if the boys were sex on legs. Which most of them were. Now I have experienced the finest of online twerking as we have already established but the Tinder pool is something else. There is less than zero depth to the "swipe and match" effect. You are basically determining your future encounters based on looks alone. So contradicting your innate set of standards as long as they have a six-pack and a nice smile. Absolute ludicrous. I was hooked. So was Kate. We spent break time comparing notes on social conquests and if we had progressed to physical contact. Which I was all over like a tramp on chips. Come on, I needed pals!

St. Patrick's Day brunch arrived. Ideal occasion to meet some cool people. And who doesn't love a shamrock gathering. Pissing rain so it was. But my only friend introduced me to a new colleague of hers…a Physiotherapist called Claire.

A FRIENDSHIP LIKE NO OTHER WAS BORN.

Claire. What a treat. More on her to come…

Also introduced to a quirky Irish poppet called Leanne, a rather charming Lebanese dude called Jad and a Canadian/Brazilian/Mentalist called Talicia. All of whom I grew to call my mates.

Leanne and I became quite close quite quickly. Only after an obnoxious encounter in Pearls and Caviar where I overheard her talk about Scottish people because she had had an argument with her fella Craig, Scottish and of course patriotic me took that out of context and got all Mohammed Ali up in her face. Poor Jad had to mediate that one and God bless him for the effort for a friendship was born the following week.

Then there was the Monte Carlo Beach club night of festivities. Organized by Jad who I had discovered championed an ex-pat Meet Up group for events for likeminded travelers. I was keen to join and meet some new folks.

Seeing Leanne there, I knew Jad would try to match us off. He had great intuition and we hit it off. What was an innocent misunderstanding giving us a giggle. Immediate friendship born and a new person to go out with! Yay for me. I had a pal. Praise the lord.

Next to her was a fine young gent, very polite and Omani. I was intrigued. His name was Tariq. Tariq was very polite and friendly. Now initially when you meet new people you think to yourself right are you going to crack on to me and do I need to be clear from the get go without sounding like an arrogant twat. Tariq very quickly established he was just one of those rare breeds of nice guys. No hidden agenda. One of my best friends in Abu Dhabi now.

Then came the crème-de-la-crème; "alright babe, what's your name then? My names Pete, Pete Wadey".

Absolute gem of a lad. Immediately creating rapping style banter with him. Like we had known each other years but equally masking this crazy "I need friends pronto and I am trying to act normal so I attract likeminded people" mantra.

And so a circle of trust was formed. We like to call it the original four. Me, Leanne, Tariq and Pete. The fab four.

Over the coming weeks, we did lots together. We were creating some amazing memories. We hit the beach, the pub, the toilet when we were so smashed we could not walk and the dance floor when Pete decided (and still decides) to teach us his individual dance moves. Rocking back and forth usually with a drink in each hand and shouting "awwwight babe".

We hit a ladies' night like little rebels only to end up in KFC at 3am on a school night. We helped lift Leanne up off the ground as she slid down the lamppost because she could barely walk.
We helped Pete eat his KFC finger licking chicken bucket after drinking one too many vodkas.
We helped each other cope. We became family. There are no other ways to describe it. They are my family. They will always be my family. I love them. Pete and Tariq are like brothers I never knew I had or would want, but are a constant support to me and encourage me to be real. Not forgetting Laura, Peters love, who is an absolute babe and when she visits it is a joy to see their love flourish.
Then there was Talicia. Meeting her at the brunch was brief. I was not enamored with her initially as I felt she was a bit subdued. I decided to ask her at a later brunch (at which point Leanne and I are spending every waking moment together god love us) and I ask her for a chat. I am glad I did.

Talicia is one of those rare breeds of delicate flowers. She is a brave soldier crusading a harsh world with traditionalist values and core morals that mean she is up against the ever-evolving world of what is deemed the norm. And she refuses to change. She refused to conform. She has little words but has huge heart. Huge compassion and an abundance of selflessness for her friends. Of which I became one on that day. And I thank my lucky stars for her. She brings me such joy. She irritates the shit out of me with her blaze approach sometimes but I would not change her and I am appreciative of the value she adds to my life, like Tariq, Pete and Leanne.

But, I have love, admiration, respect and ultimate support from my soul mate Claire Myers.

What she has done for me I will never be able to fully comprehend in words but I am going to try.

I have been blessed with amazing friends in my lifetime, granted I have had the same friends in Scotland since 2001 and I am thrilled beyond comprehension.

Living as an ex-pat in a strange country comes with it a sense of wanderlust that only fellow ex-pats understand and can feed in terms of fueling you to keep going. Claire does this for me.

I do not think she is even aware of how amazing she is. Do you know that she has single handedly rationalized my every emotional outburst, anxious episode, illness, sickness, irrational outlook to work, romance, life and everything else in between? She has a patience that must be innate for I have never seen such ability to listen with intent to just listen. Not to respond. She has proven her worth in diamonds and gold by adding immense presence in my life. Sharing experience with her is precious. A treasure she is; a friend she will always be.

We have become soul mates. Referring to each other as "wifey" we have transitioned from arguably a laughing stock prompting mockery from our growing group of friends to now just being accepted as the non-gay couple who seem gay but they are not. Even though we sometimes like to wind up the locals and the Americans at the occasional pool party that, we are indeed a couple who just happen to have an open marriage. It is HULLARIOUS. A word we penned. Then found a nail varnish with the same name and it was meant to be. She has seen her fair share of tumultuous issues whilst living in AD and I have tried to provide her with as much support as she does me. My aim was to become her person. To be her friend, sister, partner in crime. To be her person. I wanted her to call me first whenever she received good news and vice versa. It gives me hope and faith that star-crossed relationships of friendship thrive and survive on raw honesty and respect and she gives me that and more.

She calms me down when I am irrational.

She calms me down when I lose my shit unnecessarily.

She buys me kit Kat chunkies when I don't ask but then eats them both before she gets to me BUT she loves me and I her.

Claire, for the joy you bring to my life I am entirely blessed to have lived in an era where you are on my wavelength. You are a rare breed and I love you.

We have shared some of the finest and most memorable experiences of my life together. They have shaped my ability to keep the faith, even at times of great sorrow. Having had a tough 2015 with diagnosis of MS, a mild form and having some complications from chest surgery, I am thankful we have an abundance of times to reminisce on days gone by...

To name a few...

The desert safari...

Sandance Dubai...

Getting a run home in Mo's Porsche and he having his card declined at Zatar W Zeit...

Meeting Sarah Jessica Parker together dressed as night and day versions of Carrie Bradshaw and accosting her at the elevator like deranged stalkers but being equally surprised that she responded positively. Winning…

The Bahrain Grand Prix and the Gulf Air Pilot…

The many male conquests fueling our need to continuously charge our IPhone…

Our daily/momentarily, phone calls…

"Mama" (shoots self in head)

"I go to bed at night thinking about what I am going to have for breakfast"

"Here, count these 1000 AED notes, I finally got paid"

"I am always hungry"

"I am an idiot I know" HAHAHAHA

Meeting your family…

Having you be my support following my surgery…all four! Monkey face…

Maya island and the boat after parties with Hamad and his backstreet boys

Cheesecake Tuesdays

Cheesecake bread and butter

Walking around Yas Mall, any mall in fact perving on the hot Arabs

MAC lipstick

Domino's Pizza

AND the Asia De Cuba brunch…riot! I could write an entire book on tales of Kiki and Mimi.

The drive to Dubai when the car next to us pulled up a laminated sign with his number on it…HULLARIOUS

Trips to Starbucks, any bux – LOL

Cycling at Yas…

Running at Yas…

Lebanon...round one – What a laugh that was! Remember the shady room that Talicia had to negotiate the upgrade for...

Lebanon round two – Memories a plenty

FATBOY SLIM

The midget concierge...

Nick and his huge...

Veebs – LOVE HER

You. Everything you stand for, your outlook on life and your positivity, which wholly contributes to my happiness. So thank you.

Then there is the Muneera 3. Joey Deeeets, Douchebag Dave (also known as Purr of the Panther) and Kips, Tom Kips. Amazing friendships, these boys have formed with each other and I am lucky to have developed a friendship with each of them individually. In particular Tom.

Tom, thank you for being a constant advocate for my creative mind and its pressing challenges. It is not easy constructing a memoir of sorts and I know having had more than one discussion with you on how to capture articulation at its finest; you are the person I wanted to read my finished product from the very day we were introduced. Thank you for your individuality, for your support and your friendship. And thank you for helping me reach a day of completion knowing I am handing it over to the best hands I could.

Finally, not forgetting Annie. Annie, a true treasure of whimsical ways. A maternal angel gracing my life at a key moment and us both locking the door and never looking back. A friend for life.

My journey in Abu Dhabi has been a Peter Pan Never land Narnia-esque existence filled with many ups and many downs.

It allowed me freedom to express my determination in ambition as well as my striving for a better life for me.

It has seen provided a platform for me to realize my own strength and my own inadequacies. It has allowed me to develop some inner life skills I will always be thankful for. It has encouraged me to realize just what exactly I want for my life. Whilst it is merely a story so far…and whilst at the grand old age of 34 I should probably get my ovaries out of hibernation and extend the Melanie tree; the people I have met along this way have truly created the best version of me. I could go into lots of details of so many wonderful times had. I could get others and I into serious questionable discussions about their antics but that is not what this is about. This is not an expose though, more a thank you and shout out to those who have paid a particular role in the story of my life.

There are many unanswered questions residing at the forefront of my mind but they do not consume me anymore. Will I ever be skinny? Will I always fear abandonment? Will I ever find a love my heart trusts and is loyal to? Will my mother ever find the peace she so desperately wanted? Will I? Will my natural desire to forgive and accept the apology I never received remain a constant or will it peacefully fade into the abyss. I still ask myself these questions daily. But I choose to be happy. The key to my happiness? My friends and family are my fashion. They are the fundamentals of my personality and I wear their love like an accessory. Ever evolving but always present.

Sure, I have made mistakes. I have made a lot, and I have paid for them tenfold, but I have a root core of goodness. I have the time, the patience and the love for anyone crossing my path for whatever reason. I believe my written path is nourished no matter what happens.

My strength is within. I pray daily and I will continue to do so.

It serves me well to know that whilst I live my dream here, my hero, my idol, my absolute joy of a father has fulfilled his dream of becoming a stand-up comedian and he is brilliant. Brilliant in the sense of brilliance. A comic, and a humorous one at that; his wit and charm engage an audience the country over. The pride I have when watching him and hearing of him do something for *him* impacts me deeply. I know I speak on behalf of my sister and I when I say this...

Dad, you are the reason we are who we are. You are a compelling and selfless man. Your family morals and work ethics have engrained in both of us and we are wholeheartedly grateful for your sacrifices but most of all for enjoying being our dad. We love being your daughters. We adore you. You engineered a wholesome family from very little and it fuels my energy daily knowing you love me from afar.

Finally, I am settled and content in the United Arab Emirates. This country has been kind to me in many ways. I see beauty everywhere I turn and I am thankful. I wake up to the sun gracing another day and I watch the sunset over the dunes on an evening. It is pleasing for my conscious mind to know that tomorrow is always another day. And whilst perfection does not exist, I like to think I live as near to *my* perfection as I possibly can. Home is where the heart is and my heart belongs to Scotland. For now, my soul will fly amongst the dunes.

I do dream that one day I will live a harmonious and simple life in New York City. I dream of loving myself enough that I feel fulfilled in the simplicity of my surroundings. I wish to live my life through choice and not by the materialist or artificial expectations of society.

My best is good enough, my vibe attracts my tribe and I believe life is a gamble. Always back yourself to be the **winner**. Odds are in your favor and things can only get better.

The rest is still unwritten…

Fly me to the dunes

Author Profile

Melanie Hume is a 34-year old Scottish woman residing in the Middle East.

Having grown up in a single parent household, her early years tainted with overcoming raw and emotional turmoil culminating in her writing her life story as means of holistically nourishing her soul.

A keen comic, like her father, she has approached her autobiography in the most light-hearted and harmonious way, all the while, reflecting on the times that have raised an eyebrow or two.

Fly me to the dunes is her first book, her pride and joy and she is delighted to share this journey with her friends, family and budding readers.

Printed in Great Britain
by Amazon